RN

PARAMAHANSA YOGANANDA
(January 5, 1893 – March 7, 1952)

Wine of the Mystic

The Rubaiyat
of Omar Khayyam

A Spiritual Interpretation

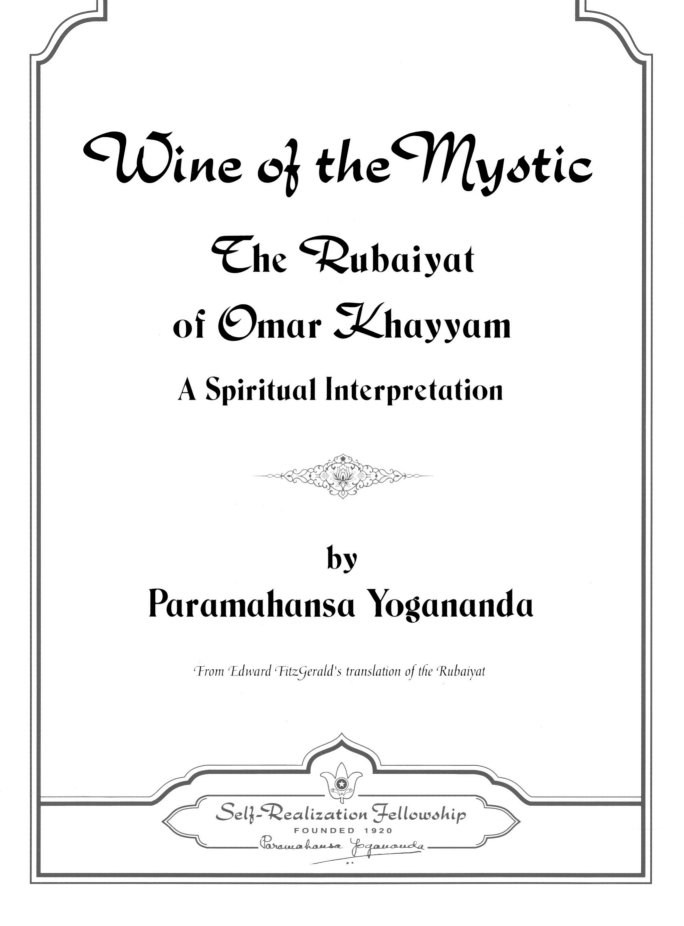

by

Paramahansa Yogananda

From Edward FitzGerald's translation of the Rubaiyat

Self-Realization Fellowship

FOUNDED 1920

Paramahansa Yogananda

A Publication of
SELF-REALIZATION FELLOWSHIP
Founded in 1920 by Paramahansa Yogananda

ABOUT THIS BOOK: Paramahansa Yogananda's spiritual interpretation of the *Rubaiyat of Omar Khayyam*, as translated by Edward FitzGerald, was originally published serially by Self-Realization Fellowship more than fifty years ago in its *Inner Culture* magazine (now known as *Self-Realization*). The series ran from 1937 through 1944. An expanded version, with additional material that had not been included in the earlier serialization, appeared in *Self-Realization* magazine from 1971 through 1990 and is being made available now for the first time in book form. Self-Realization Fellowship is pleased to present Paramahansa Yogananda's complete commentaries on this beloved literary classic.

We acknowledge with appreciation the work of artists Helen Marie, Kevin Miller, and monastics of the Self-Realization Fellowship Order who created the original illustrations and decorative borders for this book; and of Naghmeh Shaghaghi, who did the calligraphy of the Persian text of the poem.

Authorized by the International Publications Council of
SELF-REALIZATION FELLOWSHIP
3880 San Rafael Avenue • Los Angeles, CA 90065–3298

Self-Realization Fellowship was founded by Paramahansa Yogananda as the instrument for the worldwide dissemination of his teachings. The Self-Realization Fellowship name and emblem (shown above) appear on all SRF books, recordings, and other publications, assuring the reader that a work originates with the society established by Paramahansa Yogananda and faithfully conveys his teachings.

~ *First Edition, 1994* ~
Library of Congress Catalog Card Number: 94–66217
ISBN 0–87612–225–X
Printed in Singapore
11526–54321

Contents

The Spiritual Legacy of Paramahansa Yogananda

A century after the birth of Paramahansa Yogananda, he has come to be recognized as one of the preeminent spiritual figures of our time; and the influence of his life and work continues to grow. Many of the religious and philosophical concepts and methods he introduced decades ago are now finding expression in education, psychology, business, medicine, and other spheres of endeavor — contributing in far-reaching ways to a more integrated, humane, and spiritual vision of human life.

The fact that Paramahansa Yogananda's teachings are being interpreted and creatively applied in many different fields, as well as by exponents of diverse philosophical and metaphysical movements, points not only to the great practical utility of what he taught. It also makes clear the need for some means of ensuring that the spiritual legacy he left not be diluted, fragmented, or distorted with the passing of time.

With the increasing variety of sources of information about Paramahansa Yogananda, readers sometimes inquire how they can be certain that a publication accurately presents his life and teachings. In response to these inquiries, we would like to explain that Sri Yogananda founded Self-Realization Fellowship to disseminate his teachings and to preserve their purity and integrity for future generations. He personally chose and trained those close disciples who head the Self-Realization Fellowship Publications Council, and gave them specific guidelines for the preparation and publishing of his lectures, writings, and *Self-Realization Lessons*. The members of the SRF Publications Council honor these guidelines as a sacred trust, in order that the universal message of this beloved world teacher may live on in its original power and authenticity.

The Self-Realization Fellowship name and the SRF emblem (shown above) were originated by Sri Yogananda to identify the organization he founded to carry on his worldwide spiritual and humanitarian work. These appear on all Self-Realization Fellowship books, audio and video recordings, films, and other publications, assuring the reader that a work originates with the organization founded by Paramahansa Yogananda and faithfully conveys his teachings as he himself intended they be given.

— Self-Realization Fellowship

Introduction

By Paramahansa Yogananda

Long ago in India I met a hoary Persian poet who told me that the poetry of Persia often has two meanings, one inner and one outer. I remember the great satisfaction I derived from his explanations of the twofold significance of several Persian poems. One day as I was deeply concentrated on the pages of Omar Khayyam's *Rubaiyat*, I suddenly beheld the walls of its outer meanings crumble away, and the vast inner fortress of golden spiritual treasures stood open to my gaze.

Ever since, I have admired the beauty of the previously invisible castle of inner wisdom in the *Rubaiyat*. I have felt that this dream-castle of truth, which can be seen by any penetrating eye, would be a haven for many shelter-seeking souls invaded by enemy armies of ignorance.

Profound spiritual treatises by some mysterious divine law do not disappear from the earth even after centuries of misunderstanding, as in the case of the *Rubaiyat*. Not even in Persia is all of Omar Khayyam's deep philosophy understood in its entirety, as I have tried to present it.

Because of the hidden spiritual foundation of the *Rubaiyat* it has withstood the ravages of time and the misinterpretations of many translators, remaining a perpetual mansion of wisdom for truth-loving and solace-seeking souls.

In Persia Omar Khayyam has always been considered a highly advanced mystical teacher, and his *Rubaiyat* revered as an inspired Sufi scripture.* "The first great Sufi writer was Omar Khayyam," writes Professor Charles F. Horne in the Introduction to the *Rubaiyat*, which appears in Vol. VIII of "The Sacred Books and Early Literature of the East" series (Parke, Austin & Lipscomb, London, 1917). "Unfortunately, Omar, by a very large number of Western readers, has come to be regarded as a rather erotic pagan poet, a drunkard interested only in wine and earthly pleasure. This is typical of the confusion that exists on the entire subject of Sufism. The West has insisted on judging Omar from its own viewpoint. But if we are to understand the East at all, we must try to see how its own people look upon its writings. It comes as a surprise to many Westerners when they are told that in Persia itself there is no dispute whatever about Omar's verses and their meaning. He is accepted quite simply as a great religious poet.

---

* The Sufis are followers of Islamic mysticism, which the *Encyclopedia Britannica* describes as "that aspect of Islamic belief and practice in which Muslims seek to find the truth of divine love and knowledge through direct personal experience of God. It consists of a variety of mystical paths that are designed to ascertain the nature of man and to facilitate the experience of the presence of divine love and wisdom in the world." In Arabic a Sufi is also called a *faqir;* and in Persian, a *darvish*—whence the English words "fakir" and "dervish" are derived.

"What then becomes of all his passionate praise of wine and love? These are merely the thoroughly established metaphors of Sufism; the wine is the joy of the spirit, and the love is the rapturous devotion to God....

"Omar rather veiled than displayed his knowledge. That such a man would be regarded by the Western world as an idle reveler is absurd. Such wisdom united to such shallowness is self-contradictory."

Omar and other Sufi poets used popular similes and pictured the ordinary joys of life so that the worldly man could compare those ordinary joys of mundane life with the superior joys of the spiritual life. To the man who habitually drinks wine to temporarily forget the sorrows and unbearable trials of his life, Omar offers a more delightful nectar of enlightment and divine ecstasy which has the power, when used by man, to obliterate his woes for all time. Surely Omar did not go through the labor of writing so many exquisite verses merely to tell people to escape sorrow by drugging their senses with wine!

J.B. Nicolas, whose French translation of 464 *rubaiyat* (quatrains) appeared in 1867, a few years after Edward FitzGerald's first edition, opposed FitzGerald's views that Omar was a materialist. FitzGerald refers to this fact in the introduction to his own second edition, as follows:

"M. Nicolas, whose edition has reminded me of several things, and instructed me in others, does not consider Omar to be the material epicurian that I have literally taken him for, but a mystic, shadowing the Deity under the figure of wine, wine-bearer, etc., as Hafiz is supposed to do; in short, a Sufi poet like Hafiz and the rest....As there is some traditional presumption, and certainly the opinion of some learned men, in favor of Omar's being a Sufi — even something of a saint — those who please may so interpret his wine and cup-bearer."

Omar distinctly states that wine symbolizes the intoxication of divine love and joy. Many of his stanzas are so purely spiritual that hardly any material meanings can be drawn from them, as for instance in quatrains XLIV, LX, and LXVI.

With the help of a Persian scholar, I translated the original *Rubaiyat* into English. But I found that, though literally translated, they lacked the fiery spirit of Khayyam's original. After I compared that translation with FitzGerald's, I realized that FitzGerald had been divinely inspired to catch exactly in gloriously musical English words the soul of Omar's writings.

Therefore I decided to interpret the inner hidden meaning of Omar's verses from FitzGerald's translation rather than from my own or any other that I had read.*

In order to grasp readily the logic and depth of the "Spiritual Interpretations," I hope every reader will read those offerings along with the Glossary. In the "Practical Applica-

---

* FitzGerald prepared five different editions of the *Rubaiyat*. Paramahansa Yogananda, for his interpretation, chose the first edition, saying that the poet's "first inspiration — being spontaneous, natural, and sincere — is most often the deepest and purest expression." Other commentators have expressed this same appraisal of FitzGerald's various editions. For example, J. B. Rittenhouse, in an introduction to a version of the *Rubaiyat* published by Thomas Nelson and Sons in 1900, states that in FitzGerald's Second Edition, "the original renderings [were] much modified, and somewhat weakened, perhaps" and refers to the "loss of fire and verve" in the revised quatrains. *(Publisher's Note)*

tion" sections, readers who feel so inclined will find many sincere and useful suggestions as to how these truths may be beneficially applied to daily life.

Since Omar's real dream-wine was the joyously intoxicating wine of divine love, I have written, in the Addenda, a few paragraphs on Divine Love, which I received in the sacred temple of my inner perceptions. This Divine Love is what Omar advises as a panacea for all human woes and questionings.

As I worked on the spiritual interpretation of the *Rubaiyat*, it took me into an endless labyrinth of truth, until I was rapturously lost in wonderment. The veiling of Khayyam's metaphysical and practical philosophy in these verses reminds me of "The Revelation of St. John the Divine." The *Rubaiyat* may rightly be called "The Revelation of Omar Khayyam."

Foreword

This volume, presenting Paramahansa Yogananda's complete commentaries on the *Rubaiyat of Omar Khayyam*, brings together the poetic and spiritual insights of three men of great renown, whose lives spanned a period of more than nine hundred years. The eleventh-century verses of Omar Khayyam, and their nineteenth-century translation by Edward FitzGerald, have long delighted readers. Yet the true meaning of the poem has been a subject of much debate. In his illuminating interpretation, Paramahansa Yogananda reveals—behind the enigmatic veil of metaphor—the mystical essence of this literary classic.

Acclaimed for his *Autobiography of a Yogi* and other writings, Paramahansa Yogananda is widely revered as one of India's great modern-day saints. His interpretation of the *Rubaiyat* was one aspect of a lifelong effort to awaken people of both East and West to a deeper awareness of the innate divinity latent in every human being. Like the enlightened sages of all spiritual traditions, Sri Yogananda perceived that underlying the doctrines and practices of the various religions is one Truth, one transcendent Reality. It was this universal outlook and breadth of vision that enabled him to elucidate the profound kinship between the teachings of India's ancient science of Yoga and the writings of one of the greatest and most misunderstood mystical poets of the Islamic world, Omar Khayyam.

The Mystery of Omar Khayyam

In the history of world literature, Omar Khayyam is an enigma. Surely no other poet of any epoch has achieved such extraordinary fame through such a colossal misreading of his work. Beloved today the world over, Khayyam's poetry would very likely still be moldering unknown in the archives of antiquity were it not for the beautiful translations of his *Rubaiyat* by the English writer Edward FitzGerald. The paradox is that FitzGerald misinterpreted both the character and the intent of the Persian poet on whose work he bestowed immortality.

FitzGerald included in his editions of the *Rubaiyat* a biographical sketch called "Omar Khayyam: The Astronomer-Poet of Persia," in which he sets forth his conviction that Khayyam was an anti-religious materialist who believed that life's only meaning was to be found in wine, song, and worldly pleasures:

> Having failed (however mistakenly) of finding any Providence but Destiny, and any world but this, he set about making the most of it; preferring rather to soothe the soul through the senses into acquiescence with things as he saw them, than to perplex it with vain disquietude after what they *might* be.... He takes a humorous or perverse pleasure in exalting the gratification of sense above that of intellect, in which he must have taken great delight, although it failed to answer the questions in which he, in common with all men, was most vitally interested.... He is said to have been especially hated and dreaded by the Sufis, whose practice he ridiculed.

A more historically accurate portrait emerges from the research of modern-day scholars of both East and West, who have established that far from ridiculing the Sufis, Omar probably counted himself among their number. In 1941, Swami Govinda Tirtha published one of the most detailed studies of Omar Khayyam's life and writings ever made, based on a comprehensive survey of most (if not all) of the existing material on Khayyam — including biographical data from the time of Omar himself.* From that and other works of scholarship are summarized the following historical facts.

Omar's full name was Ghiyath ud Din Abu'l Fatah Omar bin Ibrahim al Khayyam. (*Khayyam* means tentmaker, referring it seems to the trade of his father Ibrahim. Omar took this name as his *takhallus*, or pen name.) He was born at Naishápur in the province of Khorastan (located in the northeastern part of present-day Iran) on May 18, 1048.† His keen intelligence and strong memory, we are told, enabled him to become adept in the academic subjects of his day by the age of seventeen. Owing to the early death of his father, Omar began searching for a means of supporting himself, and thus embarked on an illustrious public career when he was only eighteen.‡

A tract he wrote on algebra won him the patronage of a rich and influential doctor in Samarkand. Later he obtained a position at the court of Sultan Malik Shah, which included serving as the ruler's personal physician. By his mid-twenties, Khayyam had become the head of an astronomical observatory and had authored additional treatises on mathematics and physics. He played a leading role in the reformation of the Persian calendar—devising a new calendar that was even more accurate than the Gregorian, which came into use in Europe five hundred years later. Summing up Khayyam's professional achievements, Swami Govinda Tirtha tells us that Omar "was reckoned in his time second to Avicenna in sciences.§ But he combined in himself other qualifications"—having become proficient in studies of the Koran, in history and languages, astrology, mechanics, and clay modeling. (His interest in the latter pursuit is reflected in the several quatrains where he uses clay pottery and pottery-making to refer metaphorically to spiritual truths.)

After the death of Sultan Malik Shah in 1092, Omar lost his place at court and subsequently made a pilgrimage to Mecca. He then returned to Naishápur, where he apparently lived as a recluse. About the remaining decades of his life, only scanty information has survived; in particular, "over the [last] sixteen years of his life there is drawn an im-

* *The Nectar of Grace: Omar Khayyam's Life and Works*, by Swami Govinda Tirtha (Hyderabad, Government Central Press, 1941).

† Omar's date of birth has been a subject of controversy. Swami Govinda Tirtha based his assertion of the accuracy of the date given here on a thorough study of Omar's horoscope (a chart showing the position of the planets at the hour of birth), the details of which have survived in a work by one of Omar's contemporaries. Govinda Tirtha's calculations were later verified by scientists at the Institute of Theoretical Astronomy of the Academy of Sciences of the USSR.

‡ An interesting historical coincidence lies in the fact that Omar began his career in 1066 — the same year that the Norman ancestors of Edward FitzGerald, the man who would later bring worldwide fame to Omar's *Rubaiyat* through an English translation, immigrated to England as part of the army of William the Conqueror.

§ Avicenna (A.D. 980–1037), says the *Encyclopedia Brittannica*, is considered "the most famous and influential of the philosopher-scientists of Islam....Avicenna composed the *Kitab ash-shifa*, a vast philosophical and scientific encyclopedia, and the *Canon of Medicine*, which is among the most famous books in the history of medicine."

penetrable veil."* Some scholars say he spent the second half of his life pursuing the spiritual disciplines of the Sufis, and in writing the mystical poems that have survived as the *Rubaiyat.* Whether or not this is true, it is known that during this period he authored a treatise on metaphysics entitled *Julliat-i-Wajud* or *Roudat ul Qulub,* which clearly reveals his views on Sufi mysticism. Swami Govinda Tirtha, whose research indicates that this work may have been written around 1095, quotes from its conclusion as follows:

The seekers after cognition of God fall into four groups:

First: The *Mutakallamis* who prefer to remain content with traditional belief and such reasons and arguments as are consistent therewith.

Second: Philosophers and *Hakims* who seek to find God by reasons and arguments and do not rely on any dogmas. But these men find that their reasons and arguments ultimately fail and succumb.

Third: Isma'ilis and *Ta'limis* who say that the knowledge of God is not correct unless it is acquired through the right source, because there are various phases in the path for the cognition of the Creator, His Being and Attributes, where arguments fail and minds are perplexed. Hence it is first necessary to seek the Word from the right source.

Fourth: The Sufis who seek the knowledge of God not merely by contemplation and meditation [on the scriptures], but by purification of the heart and cleansing the faculty of perception from its natural impurities and engrossment with the body. When the human soul is thus purified it becomes capable of reflecting the Divine Image. And there is no doubt that this path is the best, because we know that the Lord does not withhold any perfection from [the] human soul. It is the darkness and impurity which is the main obstacle—if there be any. When this veil disappears and the obstructions are removed, the real facts will be evident as they are. And our Prophet (may peace be on him) has hinted to the same effect.

What is remarkable about this passage is not just that it unequivocally confirms Omar's Sufi sympathies, but that it expresses his spiritual goals in terms that are almost identical to those of India's ancient science of Yoga.†

Paramahansa Yogananda held that the principles and techniques of Yoga, whether or not they are called by that name, form the scientific foundation underlying the great religious traditions of both East and West. Sufi writers describe their teachings in much the same way. "Though commonly mistaken for a Moslem sect," writes the English poet and author Robert

---

* *The Cambridge History of Iran,* Vol. 4, edited by R. N. Frye (Professor of Iranian, Harvard University); published in 1975 by Cambridge University, England.

† Paramahansa Yogananda has written: "Yoga is that science by which the soul gains mastery over the instruments of body and mind and uses them to attain Self-realization—the reawakened consciousness of its transcendent, immortal nature, one with Spirit. As an individualized self, the soul has descended from the universality of Spirit and become identified with the limitations of the body and its sense-consciousness....The [Self or] soul remains essentially untouched and unchanged by its confinement in the body. But, through *maya* or delusion, it becomes subjectively identified with change and mortality, until the consciousness evolves and, through Self-realization, reawakens to its immortal state."

Graves, "the Sufis are at home in all religions....If they call Islam the 'shell' of Sufism, this is because they believe Sufism to be the secret teaching within all religions."

While a comparison of Yoga and Sufi mysticism and their sources is outside the scope of this Foreword, it is interesting to note what Robert Arnot writes in the Introduction to *The Sufistic Quatrains of Omar Khayyam:* "Khayyam's philosophical and religious opinions were in certain essential points based upon the teachings of the Vedanta. He must have been familiar with the general scope of their philosophy, although attaching himself, as we have seen, to the ranks of the Sufi mystics. In his way he was a beacon light, not only in the history of Sufi mysticism, but in the annals of God-seeking."

Similarly, the Islamic philosopher and poet Muhammed Iqbal (1877–1938), in his study of Persian metaphysics, wrote that Sufi teachers "enumerate four stages of spiritual training through which the soul has to pass if it desires to realize its union or identity with the ultimate source of all things": 1) Belief in the Unseen; 2) Search after the Unseen; 3) Knowledge of the Unseen; 4) Realization. After describing the traditional religious methods, Iqbal goes on to say that "some later Sufi fraternities (e.g., Naqshbandi) devised, or rather borrowed from the Indian Vedantist, other means of bringing about this Realization. They taught, imitating the Hindu doctrine of Kundalini, that there are six great centers of light of various colors in the body of man." He describes how the Sufi employs "certain methods of meditation" to achieve spiritual enlightenment, and cites Weber's *History of Indian Literature,* which states that by the beginning of the eleventh century the *Yoga Sutras* of Patanjali (the classic Hindu text on Yoga as a means of attaining divine perception) had been translated into Arabic, as had Sanskrit works on Sankhya (one of the six principal systems of orthodox Hindu philosophy: Mimamsa, Vaisesika, Nyaya, Sankhya, Vedanta, and Yoga).*

Whether Omar Khayyam had read these works is not known. However, according to the interpretation of his *Rubaiyat* by Paramahansa Yogananda, Omar had certainly mastered the spiritual states these works described. According to Sri Yogananda, by the time of his passing Khayyam had attained the highest goal of the yogi: complete liberation, oneness with God. (See the commentaries on quatrains 74 and 75.)

The circumstances of Omar's death, as described by his brother-in-law, seem to substantiate the concept that he was a great soul. Baihaqi, a contemporary of Omar's who recorded the tale, wrote that the poet was studying a work on metaphysics by Avicenna. When he reached the chapter on "The One and the Many," he marked the place with a gold toothpick and said, "Summon the righteous ones that I may make my testament." After this was done, he rose and prayed. His last prayer was:

> O God, Thou knowest that I have sought to know Thee to the measure of my powers.
> Forgive my sins, for my knowledge of Thee is my means of approach to Thee.

He then passed away. Govinda Tirtha places the death of the saintly poet and scientist in 1122; other scholars believe it was in 1131. His tomb is still standing at Naishápur.

* *The Development of Metaphysics in Persia,* by Muhammed Iqbal (London, Luzac and Company, 1908). The "centers of light" in the human body are called *chakras* in Sanskrit; Omar's familiarity with these and other yogic concepts is discussed in Paramahansa Yogananda's interpretation of quatrain 31.

FitzGerald and the *Rubaiyat*

Despite his achievements as a mathematician and astronomer, Omar Khayyam's name and fame would no doubt have vanished with the years had it not been for the publication of his verses by Edward FitzGerald more than seven centuries later.

"It is the *ruba'iyat* or quatrains which, mirrored in FitzGerald's masterpiece, have won for Omar the poet a fame far greater than was vouchsafed to Omar the scientist," writes Professor R. N. Frye of Harvard University. "Though not disdained by the professional poets, these brief poems seem often to have been the work of scholars and scientists who composed them, perhaps in moments of relaxation to edify or amuse — for their content can be both grave and gay — the inner circle of their disciples....Such *vers d'occasion* would at first have been transmitted only by word of mouth, but writers of the next generation or two would quote them in their works, and gradually, over the centuries, they would be collected together in anthologies, etc. This is at any rate what happened to Omar's poems. ...Of these collections the best known by far is the Bodleian MS used by FitzGerald: it was compiled in Shiraz in 1460–1 and contains 158 *ruba'is*."*

Who *was* Edward FitzGerald? He was born Edward Purcell in Suffolk, England, on March 31, 1809, of Irish parents. (FitzGerald was actually his mother's surname; his father added it to his own name in 1818.) The family was a wealthy one, and both parents claimed descent from the Norman warriors who came to England with William the Conqueror.

As a young man, FitzGerald studied at Trinity College, Cambridge, and there formed lifelong friendships with many who would become prominent literary figures of Victorian England — including Alfred, Lord Tennyson and William Makepeace Thackeray. His contemporaries described him as a shy, unassuming man who possessed great wit and charm.

Later FitzGerald became acquainted with Edward B. Cowell, respected as one of the era's preeminent scholars of Asian culture. It was Cowell who taught him to read Persian, and introduced him to Islamic poetry — including, in 1856, the then little-known quatrains of Omar Khayyam, which Cowell had discovered in a fifteenth-century Persian manuscript in the Ouseley collection of Oxford University's Bodleian Library. The following year Cowell, then serving as Professor of History at Presidency College in Calcutta, sent to FitzGerald a copy of another old Persian manuscript of the *Rubaiyat* he had come across in the library of the Bengal Asiatic Society. Not long afterward FitzGerald, working from these two sources, had completed a translation.

FitzGerald's first edition was published anonymously in 1859; it was many years before anyone knew the identity of the translator. It has been said of him that "he took as much pain to avoid fame as others did to seek it." A "Biographical Preface" that appeared in

---

* The word *rubaiyat* is the plural of the Arabic *rubai*, an epigrammatic quatrain. (Usually the first, second, and fourth lines of a *rubai* all rhyme; sometimes the third does as well.) The various surviving manuscripts of Omar Khayyam's *Rubaiyat* differ greatly in the number of quatrains they contain. Generally speaking, the later the manuscript, the more quatrains — the result, apparently, of successive copyists' incorporating into Omar's "original" the work of other poets, and perhaps their own. Thus the number of quatrains ascribed to Omar has been as low as 121 and as high as 1,200. Most scholars today estimate that no more than 250–300 are authentic.

many editions of his translation of the *Rubaiyat* after his death stated that, "he was one of the most modest men who have enriched English literature with poetry of distinct and permanent value. His favorite motto was 'Plain Living and High Thinking,' and he expresses great reverence for all things manly, simple, and true. . . . His entire career was marked by an unchanging goodness of heart and a genial kindness; and no one could complain of having ever endured hurt or ill-treatment at his hands."

A second edition of the *Rubaiyat*, revised and enlarged, came out in 1868; and further editions followed in 1872 and 1879. By the time of FitzGerald's death in 1883, he had completed five different versions.

When it first appeared, FitzGerald's *Rubaiyat* was anything but a success. Barely two hundred and fifty copies were printed, and only two journals gave it any notice, one in a review of a single sentence. The initial price of five shillings was quickly reduced, and copies of the small pamphlet were placed among the cheap books priced at a penny each. Seemingly a work destined for oblivion, it gradually began to gain the attention of an appreciative audience. Dante Gabriel Rossetti, Swinburne, and author and explorer Sir Richard Burton were among the notable figures who discovered and championed it.

Its popularity soon spread to the United States, where, owing to the lack of an American edition, "readers who caught the infection were in the habit of buying up numerous copies of the [British edition of the] book for gratuitous distribution; and where the fortuitous meeting of two strangers who were Omar-lovers immediately established a bond of close friendship."*

The Controversy Begins

As additional translations of Khayyam appeared in Western languages, controversy arose as to the accuracy of FitzGerald's presentation of the Persian poet. For one thing, when other scholars began to peruse the original, it quickly became clear that FitzGerald had taken considerable license in composing his translation — combining into one English quatrain lines from several verses of the original, and omitting many of Omar's quatrains altogether. In an introduction to a 1900 edition of FitzGerald's work, Jessie B. Rittenhouse observed: "It is certainly true that FitzGerald largely destroyed the verisimilitude of the work by giving it a continuity that does not exist in Omar. Each quatrain in the original is a detached thought, and with no consecutive arrangement other than an alphabetical one; whereas in FitzGerald there is a certain unity that has been obtained by selecting fragmentary thoughts and rendering and grouping them so as to form an Oriental poem...."

FitzGerald made no attempt to hide the fact that he had taken substantial liberties in "transmogrifying" (as he humorously put it) Omar's original into English. But he always held that he had been true to the *spirit* of the Persian poet. According to the Biographical Preface, "he maintained that, in the absence of the perfect poet, who shall re-create in his own language the body and soul of [the] original, the best system is that of a paraphrase

* Robert Graves and Omar Ali-Shah, *The Rubaiyyat of Omar Khayaam* (London: Cassell and Company, 1967), p. 17.

conserving the spirit of the author—a sort of literary metempsychosis."

Whether or not FitzGerald had really conserved the spirit of Omar Khayyam was precisely the issue. Indeed, the controversy appeared to revolve not so much around the accuracy of FitzGerald's translation as around whether or not he was correct in his conclusion that Omar was not a Sufi. The debate on this point seemed never-ending, ranging from condemnation of Omar as a materialist to condemnation of FitzGerald for ascribing atheistic views to the venerable Persian. Many who took the latter position were vehement in asserting that FitzGerald's translation could not possibly be accurate since he so grossly misunderstood the poet's intent.

On one side of the controversy were those who referred to Khayyam as "a man of rudest wit and shallowest reputation" who penned "lean and flashy songs...a tipsy toper, purblind beggar"; "a blasphemer, a poet of rationalist pessimism" whose "irreligious and antinomian utterances" were "directed against the wild ravings of the Sufis."* On the other side were those who saw a deeper symbolism in Khayyam's verse. One such was E. H. Whinfield, who in 1883 produced his own translation of Omar's quatrains, and wrote in a later book on the same subject:

> In his quatrains we constantly come across recognitions of the limitations of Science, of its inability to fathom the beginning and end of Kosmos....It is absurd to charge Omar with Materialism....Omar's revolt was only against what he regarded as the excrescences and misconceptions of religion. At bottom he was essentially religious....A man who passed a life of study and had mastered all the theology, and the philosophy and Science of the time, could hardly have been the mere sot, which a hasty reading of his bacchanalian effusions might lead one to suppose.... Sometimes he uses language which would imply entire concurrence with the rest of the Sufi doctrine, namely the spiritual intuition, the ecstasy and communion of the Soul with the One.†

The popular opinion, however, and that of most scholars, remained an echo of FitzGerald's view (though the latter acknowledged, in his second edition, the possibility that there might be some validity to the mystical interpretation of Khayyam). It was not until the 1960s that authoritative statements on the subject from a Sufi point of view appeared in the West. *The Sufis*, a 1964 study by the renowned Sufi leader and writer Idries Shah, contained an entire chapter about Omar Khayyam. In 1967, a translation of the *Rubaiyat* by Robert Graves in collaboration with the Sufi poet and scholar Omar Ali-Shah was published.‡ Working from a manuscript that had been handed down in Ali-Shah's family since the twelfth century (not

---

* Quotes cited in Omar Ali-Shah's preface to the *Rubaiyat* (see page xx).

† E. H. Whinfield, *Quatrains of Omar Khayyam* (1920), pp. vii, xiv, xv, xx.

‡ Omar Ali-Shah's family came from the region of Paghman in the Hindu Kush, where his ancestors had reigned since 1221. His elder brother is Idries Shah, author of *The Sufis* (Doubleday, 1964); the family claims the senior descent from Mohammed in Islam. Of his edition of the *Rubaiyat*, Ali-Shah writes: "The present translation is made from a twelfth-century manuscript of uncontradictable authority, whose existence has been known for centuries. I cannot claim that its one hundred and eleven verses form the complete corpus of Khayyam's *Rubaiyat*, only that these are poetically the most important ones; that they

long after Khayyam's death), Graves and Ali-Shah undertook to refute the materialistic interpretation of the poem that had been accepted by generations of FitzGerald admirers. In his introduction to that work, Graves pointed out:

> [The publication of FitzGerald's *Rubaiyat*] coincided with a strong anti-devotional movement among young English ex-Protestants encouraged in their revolt by Charles Darwin's newly broached doctrine of Evolution. As a result, FitzGerald's *Rubaiyat* became suddenly famous, and is now, for its length, the most frequent source of modern entries in English Dictionaries of Familiar Quotations.... For four generations, indeed, by an evil paradox, Omar Khayyam's mystical poem has been erroneously accepted throughout the West as a drunkard's rambling profession of a hedonistic creed: "let us eat and drink for tomorrow we die." Khayyam is also credited with a flat denial either that life has any ultimate sense or purpose, or that the Creator can be, in justice, allowed of any of the mercy, wisdom, or perfection illogically attributed to Him; which is precisely the opposite view to that expressed in Khayyam's original.

Regardless of whether FitzGerald was right or wrong in his characterization of Omar the man, he did not introduce as many new thoughts into the work of Omar the poet as some have assumed. One scholar, Edward Heron-Allen, came to the following conclusion after a careful comparison of FitzGerald's quatrains with the original Persian:

> Out of FitzGerald's quatrains forty-nine are fairful and beautiful paraphrases of single quatrains to be found in the Ouseley or Calcutta MSS or both. Forty-four are traceable to more than one quatrain, and may be termed composite quatrains. Two are inspired by quatrains found by FitzGerald only in Nicolas' text. Two are reflecting the whole spirit of the original poem. Two are traceable exclusively to the influence of *Mantiq ut Tair* of Farid ud Din Attar. Two quatrains primarily inspired by Omar, were influenced by the odes of Hafiz.

The significance of FitzGerald's familiarity with Attar, Hafiz, and other Sufi poets can hardly be overstated. As Jessie B. Rittenhouse wrote:

> His first acquaintance was with Hafiz and Sadi.... But probably from hesitancy to encroach upon the work of his friend Cowell, who was translating Hafiz, as well as from overmodesty in his estimate of himself, he did not at first attempt so ambitious a flight, but addressed himself instead to Jami... [translating the work of this Sufi poet] in a manner that merits a reading and a comment that it has not received, especially in light of its effect on the subsequent rendering of the *Rubaiyat*. In reading Jami, FitzGerald's hand was broken into his art, and the essence of the art itself so infused with his own thought that it became no longer art, but temperament, and spoke in the translation of Omar as if an original word.

This view is shared by Idries Shah. In *The Sufis*, Shah writes: "FitzGerald had become

---

all occur in one or more of the earlier MSS housed in libraries throughout the world; and that none of them is blasphemous, atheistic, or anti-Sufi in content. Finally, that Khayyam's Sufi connections form part of the oral tradition which has been handed down in my family for the last nine centuries."

soaked in Sufic teachings from what are basic Persian texts. These matured in his mind until they emerged, mixed with Omar, to form the *Rubaiyat* in English . . . . FitzGerald unconsciously maintained a Sufic impact in English literature."

Thus it is clear that by separating FitzGerald's opinion of Omar the man from his translation of Omar the poet, one comes to a more sympathetic view of FitzGerald's *Rubaiyat*. The Biographical Preface, comparing his translation with others that are more literal, concludes:

> His phrases reproduce the spirit and manner of his original with a nearer approach to perfection than would appear possible. It is usually supposed that there is more of FitzGerald than of Khayyam in the English *Rubaiyat* and that the old Persian simply afforded themes for the Anglo-Englishman's display of poetic power; but nothing could be further from the truth. The French translator, J. B. Nicolas, and the English one, Mr. Whinfield, supply a closer mechanical reflection of the sense in each separate stanza; but Mr. FitzGerald has, in some instances, given a version equally close and exact; in others, rejointed scattered phrases from more than one stanza of his original, and thus accomplished a feat of marvelous poetical transfusion. He frequently turns literally into English the strange outlandish imagery which Mr. Whinfield thought necessary to replace by more intelligible banalities, and in this way the magic of his genius has successfully transplanted, into the garden of English poesy, exotics that bloom like native flowers.

Idries Shah seemingly did not disagree, saying: "FitzGerald's version of Khayyam has never been improved upon in English because, in order for Sufi ideas to be transmitted to any extent in any generation, there must be a certain measure of harmony between the ideas and the formulation of the time. This is not to say that everyone could see this content in Omar . . . ."

It is perhaps indeed one measure of the genius of FitzGerald's translation that, like its original, it can be read on more than one level—despite FitzGerald's own belief that only a literal interpretation was valid or intended by the author. There has been an increasing willingness of scholars to acknowledge Omar Khayyam's mystical philosophy. Many have pointed out that he was using terms that were part of a metaphorical vocabulary often employed by Sufi poets. Wine for example was used to refer to the intoxication of divine love. But no interpreter in the West or the East unveiled completely the spiritual truths behind Omar's enigmatic symbolism. It was only with the appearance of Paramahansa Yogananda's interpretation that the meaning of Khayyam's imagery was fully explained.

Paramahansa Yogananda's Spiritual Interpretation of the *Rubaiyat*

It was in the early 1930s that Paramahansa Yogananda prepared his spiritual interpretation of the *Rubaiyat*. This work was first published serially in Self-Realization Fellowship's magazine from 1937 through 1944. An expanded version, with additional material that had not been included in the earlier serialization, appeared in the magazine from 1971 through 1990. With this present volume, the expanded version—containing Paramahansa

Yogananda's complete commentaries—is being made available for the first time in book form.

The Persian text of Khayyam's original appears above each of FitzGerald's quatrains. Since in compiling his translation FitzGerald often combined lines from more than one of Omar's verses (as well as introducing phrases from other sources), the Persian text will not be found to be an exact duplicate of the English. Drawing on the research of several Persian scholars, we have presented the quatrain of Omar's that most closely corresponds to each of FitzGerald's.

It is our hope that the background provided by this Foreword will help readers to enjoy more fully the depth and beauty of Omar Khayyam's immortal classic, interpreted in the commentaries of Paramahansa Yogananda. However, the various literary and historical theories about the poem and its author were not Sri Yogananda's primary interest. He would no doubt say, as did Omar himself, "Leave the wise to wrangle." His wish was not to prove or disprove a point of controversy but rather to show the way to God—the way by which each human being may find, in the ecstasy of divine love, fulfillment of every yearning of the heart and soul.

More than just a commentary, this book presents a spiritual teaching for the conduct of life. Paramahansa Yogananda reveals that behind Omar Khayyam's outward imagery is hidden a profoundly beautiful understanding of the joy and sublime purpose of human existence.

—*Self-Realization Fellowship*

WINE OF THE MYSTIC

I

خورشید کمند صبح برباماننسد کیخسرو بنوبادہ درجاماننسد
ی خورکہ منادی سحرکہ خیزان آوازه اشربوا دریاماننسد

Awake! for Morning in the Bowl of Night
Has flung the Stone that puts the Stars to Flight:
And Lo! the Hunter of the East has caught
The Sultan's Turret in a Noose of Light.

GLOSSARY—***Morning:*** Dawn of awakening from delusive earthly existence. ***Bowl of night:*** The darkness of ignorance, which imprisons the immortal soul in mortal consciousness. ***Stone:*** Spiritual discipline. ***Stars:*** The attractive twinkling of material desires. ***Hunter of the East:*** Eastern wisdom, a mighty slayer of delusion. ***Sultan's turret:*** The sovereign soul. ***Noose of light:*** The divine illumination of wisdom, which destroys the captive darkness surrounding the soul.

Spiritual Interpretation

The inner Silence sings:

"Awake! Forsake the sleep of ignorance, for the dawn of wisdom has come. Hurl the hard stone of spiritual discipline that breaks the bowl of dark unknowing, putting to flight the pale stars of mock-lustered material desires.

"Behold, the Eastern Wisdom, the Hunter and Destroyer of delusion, has caught the proud minaret of the kingly soul in a noose of Light, dispelling its imprisoning mortal darkness."

I have been inspired further to interpret this introductory quatrain as Omar's personal clarion call to the spiritually sleeping:

"O inhabitants of the City of Delusion, sleep no more! The sunlight of my awakening message of mystic wisdom has arrived. Learn how to use the hard stone of spiritual discipline to break the bowl of your dark ignorance, dashing from its hold the desire for momentarily attractive material pleasures.

"Behold with envy how the Hunter of Wisdom has been searching out and gathering the lofty, kingly, spiritually advanced devotees of Truth, encompassing their souls with a halo of the everlasting Light of Freedom."

Practical Application

Most people, though apparently awake, are really asleep in delusion. Pursued by the compelling commands of their hounding habits, they have not yet been awakened by wisdom to walk its pleasant pathways. Where life is in danger for lack of watchfulness, it is not safe to sleep. So it is unwise to slumber in the dark doorways of evil habits, which invite the danger of possible death to wisdom and true happiness.

The ordinary man earns a living, eats three times a day, amuses himself with trivial entertainments, remaining engrossed in the mechanical performance of material duties without ever awakening to the importance of understanding the purpose of life: attaining true happiness and sharing it with others. The wise man gives up false pride in self-perfection, the thought that "I am all right as I am." Using the net of introspection, he catches delusion and destroys it. Forsake the slumber of ignorant habits and awaken wisdom by performing those good habits which alone can free life from danger and crown it with lasting happiness.

To be drunk with the daily round of haunting useless habits, to be negatively the same every day for years, is a wasted experience. Destroy false pride. Awaken the soul and remain ever wakeful, striving each day to be different and better in all ways. Your soul was not meant to be a prisoner of passion, sleeping behind bars of ignorance. Jerk yourself from the stupor of sloth; race forward with progressive activities, and catch success in the net of soul creativity.

Forsake spiritual lethargy and melancholia. Bask in the light of meditative peace and Self-realization, which destroys false pride of material existence and banishes inner soul gloom.

II

Dreaming when Dawn's Left Hand was in the Sky
I heard a Voice within the Tavern cry,
  "Awake, my Little ones, and fill the Cup
Before Life's Liquor in its Cup be dry."

GLOSSARY — ***Dawn's left hand:*** Dawn of early wisdom, the first yearning to solve the mystery of life. ***A voice:*** Intuition of the soul. ***Tavern:*** Sanctum of inner silence. ***Little ones:*** Undeveloped thoughts, earliest intuitions of life's purpose. ***Fill the cup:*** Fill the consciousness. ***Life's liquor:*** Life's vitality. ***Its cup:*** The human body. ***Be dry:*** Vanish.

Spiritual Interpretation

"I had not yet fully wakened from my material sleep of ignorance, and was but dreaming of the dawn of early wisdom, when I heard the intuitive voice of my soul cry out from the tavern of inner silence: 'O little thoughts of awakening wisdom, rouse yourselves! fill the cup of consciousness with the wine of Divine Joy, ere life's vitality vanish from the bodily cup.' "

Practical Application

When man is dreaming with early inspiration, the inner voice of the soul urges him to wake up his undeveloped thoughts about the purpose of life and be practical, by filling his consciousness with true happiness—with Divine Joy—before life flies away.

The inner promptings of common sense often shake man in his mental stupor, urging him to rouse his energies and harness them for the realization of life's principal aim. Yet it is human nature that most people go on year after year dreaming wishfully that they might realize true happiness — their life's goal and foremost desire — only to find life ebbing away.

Before that comes to pass, one should take care, through determined effort, to fill the cup of his consciousness with the divinely intoxicating wine of spiritual fulfillment, and drink of that elixir to quench the thirst of life's most important desire. With the chalice of his heart he should drink smiles tapped from the hidden casks of Divine Joy he discovers daily.

III

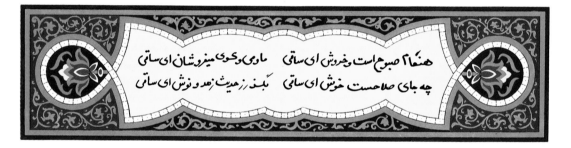

And, as the Cock crew, those who stood before
The Tavern shouted — "Open then the Door!
You know how little while we have to stay,
And, once departed, may return no more."

GLOSSARY — ***Cock:*** Wisdom. ***Tavern:*** Bodily life. ***Door:*** Portal of inner silence. ***Little while we have to stay:*** The short span of bodily life. ***Once departed:*** Having left this earth forever, after acquiring wisdom. ***May return no more:*** Need never again reincarnate.

Spiritual Interpretation

As the cock-call of wisdom sounded, delusion-drowsy devotees were aroused, and stood before the tavern of bodily life and cried, "Ah, Soul, awaken! Open the innermost door of silence, wherein lies God-consciousness. How little time we have

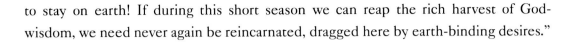

to stay on earth! If during this short season we can reap the rich harvest of God-wisdom, we need never again be reincarnated, dragged here by earth-binding desires."

Practical Application

Earthly desires are the cause of reincarnation. Souls must return life after life in new bodily forms to work out their unfulfilled cravings. But when all longings are satisfied or spiritually sublimated, there is no further need to come back to this earth of suffering and limitation.

When the first call of wisdom awakens you from the sleep of delusion, utilize the short season of earth life for cultivating reincarnation-destroying, misery-annihilating soul freedom in God-consciousness.

Everyone should make the best of his present life, for it comes but once to each soul. Even if you have to reincarnate, you will not be allowed to come a second time as the same individual. Thomas Edison can never reincarnate in the same body with the same mannerisms he had during that particular lifetime. This is true of each soul. Once we depart from the tavern of this bodily incarnation we cannot come and bide in the same fleshly tavern again. So it is the highest wisdom to make the most of this present opportunity. Follow the dictates of wisdom; listen to the voice of common sense, which urges you toward life's worthwhile goals. Open up and enliven your dormant soul faculties. Do your best to be useful to yourself and others before this ephemeral life ebbs away.

In the light of introspection, keep awake to life's highest duties and avoid the sleep-walkings of delusion and mechanical, useless actions. Honeycomb life with worthwhile activities during the summer season of opportunities. Thus you and your loved ones can enjoy sweet contentment to the end. And if by deep meditation you attain soul freedom in God-consciousness, His bliss will be yours through all eternity.

IV

اکنون که جهان را نوشی دست رسیت   هرزنده دلی اسوی سمرامو سیت
درهرشاخی طلوع موسی دستنیست   درهردشتی فرون عیسی نفسیست

Now the New Year reviving old Desires,
The thoughtful Soul to Solitude retires,
Where the White Hand of Moses on the Bough
Puts out, and Jesus from the Ground suspires.

GLOSSARY — *New year:* New dawn of wisdom. *Old desires:* The age-old longing of the soul in quest of Spirit. *The thoughtful soul:* The soul that reasons and discriminates.* *Solitude:* The inner silence of spiritual consciousness. *White Hand:* Purified consciousness. *Bough:* Universal wisdom; Christ Consciousness. *Ground:* The cosmic delusion of mortality.

Spiritual Interpretation

The awakening of new wisdom in man revives old divine desires of the soul to quest for God, and the introspecting and discriminating soul retires to the inner solitude of silence — that inner stillness in which the purified consciousness of Moses touched the bough of wisdom, and Jesus, quickened by its breath of immortality, awoke and rose from the entombing sod of delusion.

---

* Strictly speaking, the soul, being a pure reflection of Spirit, is all-knowing, and has no need to reason or discriminate. But during incarnation, the soul takes on the delusion of separation from Spirit; as wisdom begins to dawn in man through the natural upward evolution of his reason and discrimination, the soul's all-knowing faculty of intuition stirs and directs these powers within, to discover intuitively the eternal presence of the Spirit.

Practical Application

When wisdom dawns on you, awakening the desire to understand the mystery of your soul, don't put it off; retire to the inner *sanctum sanctorum* of silent peace wherein all great souls have entered, by the gate of meditation, and found wisdom and emancipation.

The thirst for understanding can be quenched only by drinking new wisdom daily from the well of discrimination. The burning desires of incarnations are alleviated only by soothing dews of peace, collected in the deep bowl of solitude. Moses, Jesus, you and I, all beings, can find the ever-sought-for solace in the silence of the soul.

This quatrain has also a mundane significance. The advent of a New Year revives old desires to succeed on the path of life. Most individuals fail to garner the rare wild blossoms of success because they do not deeply deliberate and search long enough to discover where they lie hidden in the forest of difficulties.

Everyone who seeks success, even as great men have sought it and found fulfillment, should retire often into the silence and introspect on his problems. By discrimination and meditation he can make his mind receptive to the intuitive guidance of the soul, and plan his life accordingly. Problems that have seemed insoluble will unravel their mysteries in the nook of solitary thoughtfulness.

V

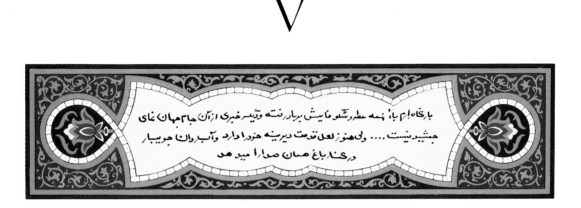

Iram indeed is gone with all its Rose,
And Jamshyd's Sev'n-ring'd Cup where no one knows;
But still the Vine her ancient Ruby yields,
And still a Garden by the Water blows.

GLOSSARY—*Iram:* Outward or sense-conscious state of man's mind and life. *Rose:* Temporary sense pleasures. *Jamshyd:* The soul's kingly consciousness of Infinity. *Sev'n-ring'd cup:* The cerebrospinal receptacle with its seven ring-like centers of consciousness and life. Through these seven plexuses the soul's life and consciousness descend from Spirit into the limitations of the body, and must ultimately ascend into the freedom of the Infinite.* *Where no one knows:* The average person is unaware of the existence of the spinal centers and of their spiritual significance. *Vine:* Soul. *Ancient ruby:* The age-old soul-bliss (the fruit or "ruby" grapes of the soul-vine). *Garden:* Self-realization, blooming with spiritual qualities. *Water:* Wisdom.

Spiritual Interpretation

When in deep meditation man withdraws his outward consciousness, there goes with it all the "rose" or pleasure associated with the senses and their desires. Yet the kingly soul consciousness of Infinity remains, engrossed within, quaffing the blissful divine consciousness from the cerebrospinal "cup," whose seven "rings" are secreted from mortal gaze and unknown to ordinary consciousness.

---

* Yogic treatises define the seven spiritual centers as *chakras* (wheels) or *padmas* (lotuses), the "spokes" or "petals" of which radiate life and consciousness to the body. The soul—the supreme Spirit, life, and consciousness in man—resides in the highest of these centers in the cerebrum, in cosmic consciousness.

As the soul's consciousness and life descend into the spine and out from the *chakras* into the physical

Unmindful of the absence of sense pleasures, such a man beholds an enthralling inner garden of Spirit, blossoming with fragrant soul qualities and sparkling with ever-flowing waters of wisdom. From the soul vine he plucks ruby grapes of Self-realization, reveling in their sweet taste of age-old ever-new Bliss.

Practical Application

By deep yoga meditation, transfer the soul's consciousness from fleshly sense pleasures to the inner spiritual perceptions of the seven cerebrospinal centers. Therein the soul intuitionally experiences the intoxicating joy of Self-realization.

In the outer sense-garden grow perfumed blossoms of short-lived pleasures, but in the inner garden of consciousness the soul secretly nurtures flowering qualities whose fragrant joy never fades. Earthly blossoms brighten man's mind for a while, but the petals of soul pleasures inspire eternally.

All the pomp and power of man's kingdom of life may fade away, and all receptacles and instruments of kingly pleasures may be taken from him; yet he can always find happiness when he roams by the healing waters of wisdom and understanding in the garden of soul-bliss.

Often, when persons fall from a state of plenty into poverty, or from success to failure, they sink in utter despair, seeing nothing to cling to. Some become so despondent they are unable to find contentment in anything. Failure cripples the subtle imagination of hope for future success. But by wisdom and discrimination man can learn that happiness is not dependent on external circumstances; rather, it is to be found in the simpler joys of life, and most of all in the ever-new bliss of deep meditation. Though destiny wrest away all earthly pleasures, man can still be happy by clinging to the simple, true, and lasting soul-joys. They come by deep thinking, introspection, spiritual inspiration, and meditation.

Gather, therefore, not only wholesome joys from the garden of material life; learn also, with your loved ones, to wander in the garden of meditation and Self-realization, and there gather the joy everlasting.

---

body and senses, its perceptions become increasingly grosser, until ultimately, in the sense-conscious state, the soul, as ego, is wholly identified with the circumscribing physical form and its limited modes of perception and expression.

Spiritual enlightenment consists in withdrawing the consciousness from the grosser states of perception to the higher spiritual centers in the spine and brain. The effect is Self-realization, or realization of the true self as Soul, made in the image of God, with all His divine qualities, reigning supreme in joy and wisdom over the kingdom of the body as well as over the heavenly kingdom within.

VI

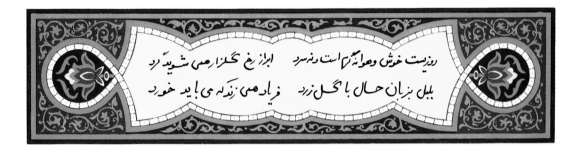

And David's Lips are lock't; but in divine
High piping Pehlevi, with "Wine! Wine! Wine!
Red Wine!"—the Nightingale cries to the Rose
That yellow Cheek of hers to incarnadine.

GLOSSARY — *David's lips are lock't:* The voice of the Infinite is outwardly silent. *High piping Pehlevi:* The lofty language of divine wisdom. As Pehlevi (Pahlavi) is the tongue of the heroic age of Persia, so divine wisdom is the language of the Infinite. *Red wine:* Spiritually vitalizing divine bliss. *Nightingale:* Intuition. As the nightingale regales man with songs at night, so in the darkness of inner silence, wherein all material phenomena are obscured, truth sings through the devotee's intuition. *Yellow-cheeked rose:* The spiritual aspirant, once rosy-cheeked and enthusiastic, whose life has paled with the severity of self-discipline and self-denial. *To incarnadine:* To crimson or vivify life with divine bliss.

Spiritual Interpretation

Though the lips of the Infinite are locked in silence, His voice is heard as the truth-singing nightingale of the aspirant's intuition, ever piping the pure language of divine wisdom. With that voice the Lord offers His devotee, grown wan with self-discipline and self-denial, the red wine of meditation's bliss, which will crimson his life with its divine vitality.

Practical Application

One who by self-control avoids intoxication by life's gross pleasures may drink the nectar of God's ever-new joy continuously from the secret cask of intuitive divine inspirations. The thirst created by self-denial is quenched fully, and in due time, by a draft of the Divine Mercy.

Foregoing unnecessary sense indulgences, the wise man develops a sensitive taste for life's finer joys, from which he imbibes enduring happiness. Such happiness lies in self-control, not in easy yieldings to mundane promptings and temptations.

Self-discipline is not necessarily self-denial, which may consist of penances in the form of extreme or unnecessary deprivations or self-torture. Self-discipline guides the moody mind in a positive way, saving it from fruitless searching for happiness in blind alleys of illusion. One who follows the way of self-discipline not only avoids dead ends in his quest for happiness, he has also the assurance of the divine law that he will be rewarded with positive success in reaching his goal. The sole purpose of self-discipline is to prevent the mind from straying off the pathway of true happiness.

Unfortunately, most mentalities are shortsighted, preferring to indulge the urgings of unthinking impulses for short-lived pleasures, rather than to exercise self-control while cultivating the fruits of life's superior joys. One who is striving to discipline his life should not grieve over the temporary deprivations of self-restraint. He should rejoice in anticipation, because self-discipline withholds happiness for but a little while, in order to bring joy that is all-fulfilling and everlasting.

The prospect of self-discipline, therefore, should not depress, but rather gladden the mind; for only through self-control can the Cosmic Law work to bring lasting happiness. As the aspiring devotee perseveres, silent God will in time speak to him through the voice of intuition, offering him the revitalizing reward of bliss for his hardships of renunciation.

VII

ازجام پیاله لبالب توبه
هر روز بر آنم که کنم شب توبه

در موسم گل ز توبه یا رب توبه
اکنون که رسید وقت گل ترکم ده

Come, fill the Cup, and in the Fire of Spring
The Winter Garment of Repentance fling:
The Bird of Time has but a little way
To fly — and Lo! the Bird is on the Wing.

GLOSSARY — *Fill the cup:* Fill your consciousness. *Fire of spring:* The warmth of spiritual enthusiasm. *Winter garment of repentance:* The soul-bliss-freezing regret that follows sense indulgence. *Bird of time:* Fleeting, ever-changing human life. *A little way to fly:* Only a little time remains. *The bird is on the wing:* Life is flying away without any definite purpose.

Spiritual Interpretation

In the warm Spring of newly arrived spiritual enthusiasm, fling off the icy garment of soul-bliss-freezing regret and repentance, created by unfulfilled material desires and disillusioning sense indulgences. Fill the cup of your consciousness with the warming wine of God's wisdom and bliss.

Waste not a precious moment, for the bird of life soars but a little while in the skies of your present existence. Behold in your mind's eye that day, how soon! it will fly away. While you have it within your power, teach this bird to sing God's all-protecting Name. Guide its flight toward His shores of immortality. Let it not sweep onward into the caverns of dark death, whither it is fast winging now without a conscious aim.

Practical Application

If you meditate deeply, you will fill your consciousness with God's all-satisfying divine wisdom and bliss. This is the positive way to overcome misery-producing temptations. What is the use of mere repentance for past follies? Do not chill the characteristic bliss of your soul with a continuous negative state of regret. Ever-awake, ever-fresh spiritual enthusiasm not only removes all depressing thoughts of past errors, but also controls the thoughts so that they do not suggest new mistakes. So do not brood over your shortcomings or despise the lack of understanding that led you to them. In the net of experience, as well as in the net of wisdom, one can catch many butterflies of worthwhile lessons—even though it is sometimes "the hard way."

The life of the ordinary man flies away swiftly and erratically. You should not ignore the opportunities, however small, afforded by your present life and intelligence. Through even the tiniest of windows, by spiritually concentrated vision you can glimpse the vast sphere of all-freeing wisdom, and the goal of all-fulfilling Bliss.

VIII

And look—a thousand Blossoms with the Day
Woke—and a thousand scatter'd into Clay:
And this first Summer Month that brings the Rose
Shall take Jamshyd and Kaikobad away.

GLOSSARY—**Blossoms:** Good and bad qualities that bloom in and around the soul. **Day:** Awakening of wisdom. **Woke:** Manifested. **Scatter'd into clay:** Destroyed by wisdom. **First summer month:** Spiritual ardor, and the ecstasy of deep meditation. **Rose:** Self-realization. **Jamshyd and Kaikobad:** The spiritual sovereignty of realized souls.

Spiritual Interpretation

Behold! a thousand buds of soul qualities bloomed with the dawn of wisdom; and in the burning rays of that dawn a thousand poisonous flowers of evil tendencies withered and were strewn in the dust. The new warmth of spiritual ecstasy* in meditation brings forth the rose of Self-realization, releasing advanced souls from earthly bondage.

Practical Application

Through many incarnations, good and evil qualities grow or fade in the ego-conscious state of the soul in its Godward evolution. Countless good and bad experiences come and go in one's life as a result of these dual qualities in his nature. But when the devotee meditates deeply and enters *samadhi* (spiritual ecstasy) the rose of Self-realization blooms in his soul, and its divine aroma of all-freeing wisdom wafts from the garden of his life. His duty as a gardener of qualities in the mortal body then ceases. The soul is released to become liberated in Spirit, free to roam happily in the eternal garden of Infinite Beauty.

To the perceptive intuition this quatrain yields yet another meaning: Everything in creation is temporal and fleeting; nothing remains permanently in this mortal sphere. Beautiful objects are like blossoms that awaken with the dawn, and die in the arms of time. The spark of life that resides in ephemeral forms, however, is immortal. This spark, the soul, evolves from life to life in an upward evolution. Whereas mortal forms are born and then fade away forever, the soul within them lives on, and comes and goes between this manifested world and the unknown void beyond. But at last, at the peak of the soul's Godward evolution, in the summer month of deep spiritual ardor and *samadhi* meditation, the rose of Self-realization blooms in the consciousness. These advanced souls are then compelled no longer to return to earth. With the death of their mortal garments they are consciously and joyously spirited away into the eternal Infinite.

* Divine communion: oneness with God.

IX

But come with old Khayyam, and leave the Lot
Of Kaikobad and Kaikhosru forgot:
Let Rustum lay about him as he will,
Or Hatim Tai cry Supper—heed them not.

GLOSSARY—*Old Khayyam:* Age-old wisdom that brings soul liberation. ***Kaikobad and Kaikhosru:*** Forgotten souls once incarnate on earth. ***Rustum:*** Potentially great soul who wastes life in temporal pleasures. ***Hatim Tai:*** The worldly-minded man who intently pursues mundane duties. ***Cry supper:*** Unthinking attachment to material activities.

Spiritual Interpretation

Follow the inner manifestation of the soul's age-old wisdom, by which emancipation can be attained. Be not discouraged by the sad destinies of forgotten souls who have come and gone on earth. Mourning their lot will not save you from a similar fate. Let others while away life's precious time in worldly pleasures, or in slavishly pursuing material duties; but do not imitate their ways. They reap a harvest of disillusionment and death.

Practical Application

How many souls have come on earth, only to slip away into the secret silence! Never mind. Leave to their folly those who are indolent or engrossed in mundane life. Let not sadness or attachment hinder the progress of your soul. Follow the ancient wisdom that leads to soul emancipation, heeding not the relativities, dualities, and complexities of this existence; for life is nothing but a Cosmic Dream.

There are moody metaphysicians who like to philosophize over the dismal fate of souls and of civilizations, which now and again bloom on this earth with great pomp and splendor, only to droop in the hot breeze of death. Brooding over the temporality of this world, these metaphysicians turn up their noses at all materially beautiful things just because they must someday perish. But nothing is gained either by disdaining the beautiful creations of civilization, or by gloomily dwelling on the fate of man and his accomplishments. Wisdom alone offers solution to the conundrum of life.

Behind brittle walls of false material security, the opulently rich and powerful while away their time and roam the pleasure fields of delusion, heedless of approaching death.

Like automatons, ordinary worldly-minded people eat breakfast, lunch, and supper with rigid regularity, and, in between, painstakingly pursue their material duties; yet they die dissatisfied and disheartened. Like the gold-laden mule, they laboriously carry the burden of daily duties, unaware of the value and opportunities of life. Eventually they become lost in the hopelessness of old age and the unhappy prospect of oblivion.

The divine philosopher is the truly happy man. A spiritual poet, he uses his imagination to envision the immortality of the soul-image of God in all beings. With faultless gaze he peers through the windows of ever-changing physical forms and beholds God's changeless beauty.

Therefore, lament not over destiny, nor laze away life's golden hours in useless pastimes, nor follow this material existence insensible of its purpose. Cultivate in yourself God's age-old, ever-new wisdom, which alone gives lasting happiness, ultimate contentment, and soul freedom.

X

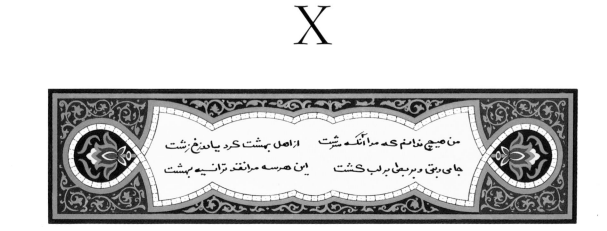

With me along some Strip of Herbage strown
That just divides the desert from the sown,
*   Where name of Slave and Sultan scarce is known,*
And pity Sultan Mahmud on his Throne.

GLOSSARY — ***Strip of herbage:*** Narrow plot of superconsciousness, the soul's ever-new wisdom, hidden between subconsciousness and waking consciousness. ***Divides:*** Subtly separates. ***Desert:*** The desolate subconscious mind, where the fresh daily experiences of the conscious mind are lost and buried. ***The sown:*** Atmosphere of material civilization cultivated by the conscious mind. ***Slave:*** Subject to instincts, illusions, and distractions of the subconscious mind. ***Sultan:*** Powerfully developed material consciousness. ***Pity Sultan Mahmud on his throne:*** Feel compassion for those who vainly seek happiness in temporal power.

Spiritual Interpretation

Heed the call of your soul to search out that hidden place where fresh evergreen plants of wisdom separate the desolate desert of delusion from the cultivated fields of material consciousness, and bad from good karma (actions).

Remember: the karmic law of cause and effect governs all men, whether slaves or kings. The most powerful emperor cannot escape the painful effects of his ignorant or wrong actions. You may be indifferent to your past actions and forget them, but they will not forget you, no matter what your station in life.

Therefore, by discrimination free yourself from harmful tendencies created by deluded thoughts and actions in the past and buried in the subconscious mind; and avoid further wrong thoughts and actions by the conscious mind under the influence of material culture. Place your consciousness in the cradle of perfection: the intuitive superconscious wisdom of your soul.

Practical Application

Every truth-seeker should strive for the self-rejuvenating, ever-fresh, ever-inspiring state of divine superconscious wisdom, which lies hidden between the untracked desert of subconsciousness and the cultivated fields of the highly organized waking consciousness. By introspection on the joyous state of deep sleep,* and by going into the silence daily in deep meditation, the devotee reaches consciously the state of all-satisfying superconscious wisdom. He is then free from slavery to instinct and moods and habits hidden in the subconscious mind, and free also from the influence of powerful material desires created in the conscious mind.

Happy are those who are wise enough to seek contentment by cultivating true joy and peace in a simple environment — a place that is neither a dreary waste nor a cultivated center of restless, driving, artificial living. Those who keep their life uncomplicated, and do not depend on material conditions for their happiness, possess more than the rich and powerful, who want for happiness amid material plenty and are friendless among self-seeking friends; who are lonely even in a crowd, and joyless amid false pleasures. A wealthy potentate, in useless pursuit of lasting happiness through short-lived worldly pleasures, may well be pitied by that devotee who has gained the eternal satisfaction of superconscious wisdom: the realization of his own Self, the ever-existing, ever-conscious, ever-blissful image of God.

* In deep sleep, man subconsciously feels the superconscious joy of the soul, which is crowded out during the ordinary dream state and the mentally busy wakeful state.

XI

وزیک دوشی زکوسفندی رانی   کردست دمه زنغز کندم نانی

عیشی بودان نه هڱهرسفانی   بامامنی نشته دربرانی

Here with a Loaf of Bread beneath the Bough,
A Flask of Wine, a Book of Verse—and Thou
Beside me singing in the Wilderness—
And Wilderness is Paradise enow.

GLOSSARY—***Bread:*** *Prana,* or life force (cosmic life energy). ***Beneath the bough:*** With attention inwardly concentrated on the cerebrospinal tree of consciousness (whose trunk is the pranic pathway of life into the body, and whose branches are the nervous system). ***Wine:*** God-intoxication; the bliss of divine love that comes when one communes with God in meditation. ***A book of verse:*** Inspirations of divine love emanating from the heart. ***Thou:*** God, the Cosmic Beloved. ***Singing:*** Entertaining with intuitional perceptions of sublime truth. ***In the wilderness:*** In inner silence, whence crowds of restless thoughts have departed. ***Wilderness is paradise:*** The initial loneliness felt in the stillness of deep meditation, owing to the absence of restless thoughts, becomes a paradise to the devotee when he discovers therein the celestial bliss of God.

Spiritual Interpretation

In this quatrain the devotee is describing the deep state of God-communion attained through *pranayama,* control of mind and life force *(prana).**

---

* Referred to in this quatrain as "bread," or the sustainer of life; cosmic life energy felt in the cerebrospinal tree of life through *pranayama,* control of mind and life force by means of scientific techniques of meditation. When one is eating, attention is concentrated in the palate; when listening, in the ear; and during meditation and divine communion, attention is concentrated in the *chakras* (six spiritual centers of con-

"Sitting in the deep silence of meditation, with my mind concentrated on the cerebrospinal tree of life and spiritual consciousness, I rest in the shade of peace. Nourished by the life-giving 'bread' of *prana*, I quaff the aged wine of divine intoxication brimming the cask of my soul. Unceasingly my heart recites the poetic inspirations of eternal divine love. In this wilderness of deepest innermost silence—whence all tumult of thronging desires has died away—I commune with Thee, my Supreme Beloved, the Singing Blessedness. Thou dost sweetly intone to me the all-desire-satisfying music of wisdom. Ah, wilderness, free from the clamor of material desires and passions! in this aloneness I am not lonely. In the solitude of my inner silence I have found the paradise of unending Joy."

Practical Application

Neither human love nor the temporary oblivion of intoxication by wine can permanently erase sorrow and yield lasting happiness. The attainment of unending unalloyed joy is possible only by communing in deepest meditation with the Supreme Beloved of the Universe, as described in the spiritual interpretation of this quatrain.

But when grief and difficult problems beset the good worldly man, he can learn to find contentment and refreshment in the simple joys of life. The beauty and serenity of nature, enjoyed in the company of one's truly beloved and sympathetic spouse; the satisfaction in wholesome savory food and drink (the fresh juice of the grape is nonintoxicating, and less costly!); the upliftment of inspirational books — through such simple pleasures one learns to appreciate unsophisticated happiness. Joy flies away when multifarious conditions are imposed upon it. Some never find happiness, no matter how many material possessions they have; they are always desiring something more. Those who find happiness easily are those who realize that happiness does not depend on acquiring unnecessary "necessities."

---

ciousness located in the spine and medulla) and at the spiritual eye (the point of intuitive spiritual perception, between the eyebrows).

Practicing the yogic science of *pranayama*, the deeply meditating devotee withdraws his attention from the restlessness of the body and its five instruments of sensory perception and interiorizes his mind in the cerebrospinal centers of spiritual consciousness. These *chakras*, in ascending order from the base of the spine, form a pathway through which body consciousness is uplifted to soul-realization and ecstatic God-communion. In this state of divine recollectedness, the soul experiences pure Bliss. The *prana*, or life force, previously dissipated in sensory perceptions and bodily restlessness, is brought under conscious control, vitalizing all the bodily cells. The refreshment thus experienced is unequaled by that obtained from sleep, or food, or any other material source.

If a person is forced by circumstances to give up a wealthy, materially complex life for a relatively poor and simple one, he should make the best of it. To allow his happiness to vanish along with his evanescent riches would be to mistakenly equate happiness with material advantages. If he tries his utmost, he will have a better chance of finding true happiness in his new situation than in the life he led before.

After failure to attain a cherished goal, the heart may become like a desolate wilderness, devoid of any fresh herbage of hope. But if the unsuccessful man appreciates what he does have—the simple joys of life, and perhaps a true soul companion—then even in the desert waste of temporary failure he finds an oasis of lasting inner celestial happiness.

XII

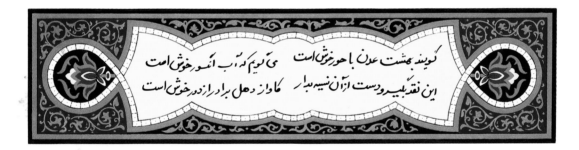

"How sweet is mortal Sovranty!"—think some:
Others—"How blest the Paradise to come!"
Ah, take the Cash in hand and waive the Rest;
Oh, the brave Music of a distant Drum!

GLOSSARY— *Mortal sovranty:* Temporal material powers. *Paradise to come:* Uncertain hope for future happiness. *Cash in hand:* Tangible wealth of imperishable soul wisdom and ever-new divine bliss found in meditation. *Waive the rest:* Forgo the pursuit of unnecessary "necessities." *Brave music:* Joyful thoughts of confident expectancy. *Distant drum:* Assured hope of future success that comes with living rightly by acquiring wisdom first.

Spiritual Interpretation

Some materialists feel secure in their intoxication with worldly powers and possessions. Many others cling to a frail happiness as they chase the rainbow of uncertain hope that someday their dreams will come true. It is folly to expect lasting joy from temporal things or from ever-eluding worldly hopes. But imperishable tangible wealth is already yours: the ever-new divine bliss of soul wisdom. It lies within your power, in deep meditation, to claim this treasure from the abiding altar of ever-solacing soul contentment. Cease groping after the deceptive will-o'-the-wisp of material attainments promised by a fickle future. Acquire now the supreme wisdom that bestows bliss. There is no greater happiness than divine joy, which is ever new. And those who make wisdom their wealth now, while the sun of spiritual opportunity shines, will always receive encouraging joyous intuitions of future grand attainments. Hearing within their souls the resounding drum of Omnipotence, they know that divine power is theirs to acquire at will whatever they need, and to realize all future bright hopes of eternal happiness.

Practical Application

The precious time allotted in this life is squandered by some people in impossible foolish dreams of acquiring wealth and the sweet happiness it is supposed to give. It is unwise to trust material wealth as bestower of lasting joy. Those who anchor all their hopes for happiness on the acquirement of riches, and utterly forget the art of realizing true inner divine bliss, ultimately find that their faith in the temporarily satisfying qualities of material possessions is completely shattered. Happiness cannot be found in a disorganized life that does not balance material pursuits with spiritual necessities. He whose concentration is scattered in moneymaking ambitions only, continues to feel restless unfulfillment in his soul, his true self. Octopus habits of peace-destroying worry accompany avid desire for wealth. After a time, such habits refuse to release their tenacious hold or to be displaced by peace and contentment. On the other hand, simple living and the acquirement of soul peace and joy bring an all-satisfying happiness undreamed-of by the materialist. Material possessions alone cannot make life secure; one is truly safe only if he has also found within his soul the Cosmic Security.

XIII

خنلان خنلان سربه جهان آوردم   کل کفت کدست زرنشان آوردم

هرنقه کبود درمیان آوردم   بنازسرکیسه برسرفتم رنتم

Look to the Rose that blows about us — "Lo,
Laughing," she says, "into the World I blow:
At once the silken Tassel of my Purse
Tear, and its Treasure on the Garden throw."

GLOSSARY — *Look:* Analyze. *Rose that blows about us:* Material pleasures that surround us. *Laughing, into the world I blow:* Mocking, on every breeze I waft the temptation of sensory pleasures. *Silken tassel of my purse:* Attachment to the senses, which binds man to worldly experiences. *Tear:* Cut off by wisdom. *Its treasure on the garden throw:* Fling its false pleasures on the earth.

Spiritual Interpretation

Fragrant and short-lived as the rose, the pleasures of materiality mock human beings who do not understand their ephemeral nature. Delay not that understanding, lest you be trapped in the enfolding pleasure-petals, entombed like the bee that tarries too long in the lotus closing at sunset.

Tear asunder with wisdom the stem of attachment that holds together your prison of passing-pleasure petals. Fling them underfoot and press forward through the garden of life on your pathway to Infinity.

Practical Application

Most mortal beings who come into this world are like the roses that blow in the garden; after a brief, materially pleasurable existence, they shed the petals of their lives in the oblivion of death. Such a meaningless existence cannot satisfy man. He should fully employ his God-given life in the acquirement of liberating wisdom, that he may banish forever the delusion of material happiness and find within himself the ever-conscious, ever-existing, ever-new joy of the soul.

In the chamber of introspection, analyze the temporal, dissatisfying nature of the sense pleasures—gaudily promising outwardly, but inwardly empty. By close scrutiny you will discern how the impermanence of sense delights mocks you. You will realize that you would be better off without these unstable rosy pleasures that abound in material life. With this realization comes a desire to tear away their sustaining stem— your attachment to them. If, strengthened by wisdom, you are able to do this, you will easily discard your false imaginings about the value of material pleasures, and you will cast from your consciousness all desire for them.

It is only by deep discrimination that one understands the unworthy nature of material desires and becomes able to tear them away from the heart. The prudent man cultivates discrimination. But anyone who remains addicted to sense pleasures long enough cannot but realize, finally, their fickle nature and the necessity of freeing the soul from their imprisoning roots.

XIV

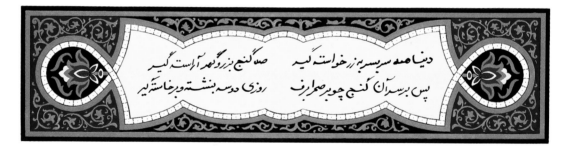

The Worldly Hope men set their Hearts upon
Turns Ashes—or it prospers; and anon,
*   Like Snow upon the Desert's dusty Face*
Lighting a little Hour or two—is gone.

GLOSSARY—*Worldly hope:* Expectation of gaining earthly happiness. *Men:* Materially minded people. *Set their hearts upon:* Foolishly become attached to. *Turns ashes:*

Reduced to dust by the fires of disillusionment. *Or it prospers:* Is fulfilled briefly. ***Like snow upon the desert's dusty face:*** Evanescent worldly happiness, disappearing in the face of disillusionment. ***Lighting a little hour or two—is gone:*** Imparting a little tantalizing delight, then vanishing.

Spiritual Interpretation

Worldly hope is a deceiving will-o'-the-wisp, luring unsuspecting pursuers to their doom. Yet just as the short-lived snow is momentarily pleasant and soothing on a hot, dry desert, so even short-lasting successful fulfillments of our desires are for a little while alluringly comforting. Fools, enticed by passing pleasures, continue to wander in the desert of earthliness. The wise, even while enjoying evanescent prosperity on earth, do not forget the imperfect nature of the world—the crematory ground of delicate dreams. Only the ignorant man expects perfection and lasting fulfillment from this earth; and brokenhearted he enters the portals of the grave. The enlightened man, knowing the delusive nature of the world, does not build his hopes here. Remaining unmoved by earthly desires, the wise seek the lasting Reality; they enter the vastness of Eternal Fulfillment.

Practical Application

The light of discrimination reveals that shadowy hopes of earthly happiness usually end in disillusionment, affording only now and then a temporary fulfillment. It is the occasional successes, short-lived though they be, that lure people to go on trailing material desires. But the joy of temporary success ends in disappointment; it evaporates all too quickly, like a flake of snow on warm desert sands. Therefore it is unwise to spend so much time and energy to achieve mundane happiness. Toil for blessedness, which lasts forever. Most human beings spend their life's time in acquiring possessions and fulfilling ambitions that give impermanent happiness. At the end of life they are often disheartened and bewildered, wondering why their hard-won happiness did not last.

Neither plunge into boisterous excitement when fickle fortune visits, nor become benumbed with fear when invaded by temporary failure. Prosperity and poverty are significant only in relation to physical well-being; their importance vanishes with the perishable body. When compelled to ride the ups and downs of life's successes and failures, try to maintain a balanced mental peace. We can control our contentment when we are evenly peaceful at all times.

Through meditation one can experience a stable, silent inner peace that can be a permanently soothing background for all harmonious or trialsome activities demanded by life's responsibilities. Lasting happiness lies in maintaining this evenly peaceful state of mind, even when worries seek to unsettle the inner equanimity, or success tries to excite the mind to abnormal elation.

A lump of sand cannot withstand the erosive effect of the ocean's waves; an individual who lacks imperturbable inner peace cannot remain tranquil during mental conflict. But as a diamond remains unchanged no matter how many waves swirl around it, so also a peace-crystallized individual remains radiantly serene even when trials beset him from all sides. Out of the changeful waters of life, let us salvage through meditation the diamond of unchangeable soul-consciousness, which sparkles with the everlasting joy of Spirit.

XV

زان پیش که بر سرت شبیخون آرند   فرمای که تا باده گلگون آرند

تو زر نه ای غافل نادین که ترا   درخاک نهند و باز بیرون آرند

And those who husbanded the Golden Grain,
And those who flung it to the Winds like Rain,
Alike to no such aureate Earth are turn'd
As buried once, Men want dug up again.

GLOSSARY—*Golden grain:* The idol of wealth. ***Husbanded:*** Hoarded. ***Flung it to the winds:*** Spent wantonly. ***Alike:*** Miser and spendthrift are equally deluded. ***To no such aureate earth are turn'd:*** Not to gold, but to dust, is man's clay transformed at death. ***Buried once, men want dug up again:*** Attachment to material life makes man long to return to the physical form.

Spiritual Interpretation

Why, O Man, should you exalt gold, either to hoard it for security or to spend it extravagantly for luxuries? Give scant consideration to the desires of the physical body, to which wealth seems so sweet, since all mortal frames must shortly return to dust, valueless for any purpose.

Practical Application

If one makes gold his idol, there is little difference, metaphysically, whether one guards it like a miser or enjoys it like a spendthrift: both courses proceed from the delusion that wealth is the supreme source of happiness. He who glorifies money is erroneously identifying his Self with the physical body, for which he desires the security and comforts of wealth.

How foolish is man to identify his immortal consciousness with the perishable human form, which death renders inert and destitute of all desirable qualities! Indeed, considered as matter, our dull clay cannot compare with the gleaming ore that men rescue eagerly from the earth.

A deeper metaphysical meaning is also to be found in this quatrain. It refers to life in general, and, in particular, to cultivation of the intellectual wisdom required to make the most of life's opportunities; and to man's bondage to this earth through the law of reincarnation, which is activated by unfulfilled desires.

Man's material desires and aspirations lead him to fancy this earth as a place of fulfillment and ultimate happiness. Thus, most people want their interrupted life "dug up again"; they would like to be able to return from the grave in the same dear form to which they are so attached, and to continue with the same familiar life—minus, of course, its trials and disappointments! But neither those beings who make the most of life and attain material success by nurturing the "golden grain" of intellectual wisdom, nor those who remain dullards and cast this life to the winds of lost opportunity —as rain is blown by the breeze—can return to earth with the same name, opportunity, or form. Return they do, according to the law of reincarnation, but with a new brain and body, to complete the lessons of this school of earthly existence. Repetition of shunned earthly experiences, incarnation after incarnation, is inevitable if the soul is still bound by mortal consciousness and longings when it leaves for the beyond.

However, man's return is "to no such aureate earth" as mortal desires lead him hopefully to envision. He will never find this world a haloed heaven. Since it is impossible to repeat this particular life, once it is lost to us, we should make the most of present opportunities to cultivate not only intellectual success-giving wisdom, but imperishable soul wisdom. Once Eternal Life is gained, one craves no longer to reenter the lost temporary bodily dwelling.

XVI

این کهنه رباطی که عالم نام است   آرامگه ابلق صبح و شام است
بزمی است که وامانده صد جمشید است   قصری است که تکیه گاه صد بهرام است

Think, in this batter'd Caravanserai
Whose Doorways are alternate Night and Day,
How Sultan after Sultan with his Pomp
Abode his Hour or two, and went his way.

GLOSSARY — *Batter'd caravanserai:* The woesome tavern of this world, ravaged by recurring storms of human sorrows and natural catastrophes. ***Whose doorways are alternate night and day:*** The recurrent cycles of life and death, reminding us of our unknown cosmic environment. ***Pomp:*** The grandiose delusion that prevents man from fully accepting the fact that his present life and power must end in death. ***His hour or two:*** Man's short life, as compared to Eternity.

Spiritual Interpretation

This worn and ancient world is but a stopping place whose doors are alternating birth and death. Reflect that many monarchs with splendid courts, proud families, and mighty powers have tarried here awhile, only to be snatched into the secret chamber of death.

The lifespan of the moth seems momentary, compared to our own. So is each human life but a brief flickering before the eternal eyes of God. Both the iridescent moth and the resplendent sovereign make their entrances and exits right before our eyes; yet our own pompous delusions of security make us quickly forget that we likewise come and go before God's changeless gaze.

Strangest of all truths — though everybody dies, yet so long as we live, we can never picture in our minds that we too shall drop like dried petals on the tract of the unknown mystery.

Practical Application

One should not become complacent in the uncertain security of a healthy, materially prosperous life, and thus neglect to seek the saner, more worthwhile pursuits that yield lasting happiness. Powerful people have been crumbled to dust without a moment's notice. Follow the path of wisdom. By scientific yoga meditation, establish your palace of peace on the rock of ages, the indestructible inner peace of God.

XVII

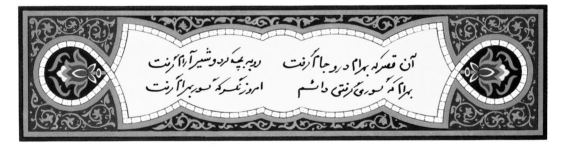

They say the Lion and the Lizard keep
The Courts where Jamshyd gloried and drank deep;
And Bahram, that great Hunter — the Wild Ass
Stamps o'er his Head, and he lies fast asleep.

GLOSSARY — ***The lion and the lizard keep the courts:*** Eventually the animals, from the greatest to the least, reign over the ruins of man's broken monuments of worldly triumph. ***Jamshyd:*** Famous Persian sultan; symbol of temporal power. ***Bahram:*** Sassanian sovereign of Persia, noted for his cruel persecution of Christians, and for his prowess as a hunter. ***The wild ass stamps o'er his head:*** The hunted mocks the hunter, demonstrating the impartiality of nature, which allows time to bring about the reversal of all material power and the felling of mortal pride. ***Lies fast asleep:*** The once-great power is rendered powerless by death.

Spiritual Interpretation

Only the lowly animals roam and rule the deserted city where once King Jamshyd gloried in the splendor of his court. He drank to the full of material pleasures, vainly boasting all the while that he was an immortal. But even proud kings bow at last to the dust, and the mighty monuments of their power are mocked by the indifference of man and beast, who trample the sites of their thrones. The audacious wild ass frolics without fear over the grave of the once-dreaded hunter, Bahram; his power, too, now sleeps in impotence. Similarly must all men relinquish their imposing domains, yielding them to greater or lesser powers; for worldly glory is unstable, and material achievements, pomp, and riches are fleeting.

Practical Application

Time destroys all earthly greatness; even the strongest body succumbs at last. From this common fate of all who have lived before our little time, we should learn that we too, whether great or insignificant, eventually have to share the same end. The *danse macabre* tramples into dust all material creations. Therefore we should not become engrossed in earthly glory, opulence, or power; for each life is only a temporary role we play on the stage of time. This part may be finished at any moment, for sooner or later the curtain will close on the present scene. The parts we play on earth have only the play's temporary reality. Play well, but mind the Director; and do not become identified with and attached to that which is impermanent. The ego dies, and with it all its pride. That which survives immortally is the humility of the soul, which brings God's blessings and the lasting realization of the peace and joy of God Himself.

XVIII

درمر دشتی که لاله زاری بو دست   آن لاله زخون شهر باری بو دست
هر برگ بنفشه کز زمین می روید   خالیست که بر رخ نگاری بو دست

I sometimes think that never blows so red
The Rose as where some buried Caesar bled;
That every Hyacinth the Garden wears
Dropt in its Lap from some once lovely Head.

GLOSSARY — *Never blows so red:* Never so well reflects how all creation is interlinked. *Hyacinth:* Noble thought. *Garden:* The human mind. *Lovely head:* Inspiring soul.

Spiritual Interpretation

Redder seem the roses that grow in a soil steeped with the blood of a Caesar, for in the eye of the beholder their beauty enlivens the memory of the greatness of that Caesar's soul. Even the blossoms are unconsciously conscious of that kingly life. It is a truth that the actions of man influence other created objects; and he, in turn, is influenced by his environment.

So also are the minds of men interlinked. Every blossoming hyacinth of noble thought grown in the garden of human mind is an offshoot from the wisdom brain of some lovely soul. For none of man's thought discoveries is entirely original; all were inspired either by the wisdom of others, or by the One Cosmic Wisdom: the inexhaustible Fountainhead of all human intelligence.

Practical Application

The reddest roses of man's remembrance—deeply tinged with tenderness, mystery, and sympathy—are for heroic souls, long-passed from the garden of life. These thought-blossoms lend continuing enchantment to the memory of such lives, perhaps romanticizing them even more than their achievements deserve.

Yet it is wise to recall the renowned, for they inspire us to strive for greatness. Every noble quality that has flowered in the garden of men's minds and actions has come from the inner loveliness of the soul. Ponder the soul; for it is the source of all our inspirations for material, mental, and spiritual success.

XIX

And this delightful Herb whose tender Green
Fledges the River's Lip on which we lean—
Ah, lean upon it lightly! for who knows
From what once lovely Lip it springs unseen!

GLOSSARY—*Delightful herb whose tender green:* Subtle sensations, and the thoughts and perceptions they create. ***The river's lip on which we lean:*** The river of life, flowing through the cerebrospinal centers, on which man's vitality and awareness depend. ***Lean upon it lightly:*** With the keenness of intuition, far more delicate than sense perception, concentrate on the cerebrospinal centers of life. ***What once lovely lip:*** The perfection of God manifested in man as individualized soul, so lovely at its Source before it descends into the grossness of physical expression. ***It springs unseen:*** From this unseen Source, all life flows forth.

Spiritual Interpretation

Through the caverns of the seven subtle centers in the spine and brain flows the astral river of life, on which the vitality and awareness of all human beings depend.* On the banks of this river, springing from subtle nerve centers in the spine,

---

* Man's astral or subtle body of light (intelligent energy) is the second of three sheaths that successively encase the soul: the causal body (idea-matrix for the astral and physical bodies), the astral body, and the physical body. The powers of the astral body enliven the physical body, much as electricity illumines a bulb. The astral body has nineteen elements: intelligence, ego, feeling, mind (sense-consciousness); five instruments of knowledge (the sensory powers within the physical organs of sight, hearing, smell, taste, and touch); five instruments of action (the executive powers in the physical instruments of procreation, excretion, speech, locomotion, and the exercise of manual skill); and five instruments of life force that perform the functions of circulation, metabolization, assimilation, crystallization, and elimination.

51

grow the green herbs of all human sensations, which give rise to fresh thoughts and perceptions. Thus all experiences of life on the physical plane rest on the cushion of astral sensations.

While enjoying outwardly the physical expression of the senses, be not unconscious inwardly of the river of life gliding through the cavernous astral cerebrospinal grotto, nor of the fine perceptions adorning its banks. With gentle intuition born of meditation, feel the subtle spinal perceptions flowing from the unseen Fountain of Life and Consciousness in the brain.

Practical Application

Man's five sensory powers spring from the astral river of life in the spine, and are themselves astral in nature. The sensory organs of the body are the instruments through which these astral powers receive the vibrations of the grosser physical plane and relay them to the brain for interpretation and response. As man learns to concentrate and take his consciousness within in meditation, he becomes aware of the inner river of intelligent life energy and consciousness that flows through the spiritual centers in the spine from its source in the brain. In that deeper awareness he realizes the true subtle nature of his senses, and how much finer and keener their perceptions are when freed from the limited physical-body instrument.

The mind of the ordinary person is usually engrossed only in the sensations of sight, sound, taste, smell, and touch, coming to him from the surface of the body. Constant experience of these physical sensations entraps the mind in physical consciousness. Those who love attractive words of flattery become lost in the labyrinth of the ear. The slave of beauty is locked in the twin caves of the retinae; the gormandizer is a prisoner of the palate. Addiction to alluring aromas, and inordinate attraction to that which is pleasant to the touch, are other forms of perpetual bondage to body consciousness. Man thus remains oblivious of the finer perceptions in the spine, which would lead him to awareness of the soul, his true nature.

The senses function through the mechanism of the nervous system, in a manner comparable to the transmission of telephone messages. During waking consciousness, the mind of the ordinary person is busy madly conversing with the senses through the five sense telephones on the outer end of the connection. He never knows that at the inner end in the subtle center of divine consciousness in the brain, beyond the insulated spinal canal,* are the unseen lips of Spirit, whose voice speaks to him through his soul and imbues his nervous system with vitality.† This vitality, or intelligent life force, is the medium through which the soul and the senses exchange their experiences.

As man is identified with the senses or body consciousness during wakefulness, and becomes one with the subconscious state during sleep, so, in deep meditation he turns his attention inward, and concentrates on the peace and joyous perceptions of superconsciousness in the subtle cerebrospinal centers, especially those in the heart and brain. In the superconscious state he becomes aware of the intelligent life forces and soul consciousness inside the body, instead of dwelling only on the sensory surface of the body. By cultivating this inner communion with the consciousness of his true self, the soul, man can escape his slavery to the body and all its sufferings. Becoming established in his divine nature, he can enjoy life as never before, experiencing the beauty and sweetness of the Divine Loveliness behind all physical sensations.

* The *sushumna* or spinal sheath that encloses the astral river of life.

† Entering the brain at the medulla, the cosmic intelligent vibration (here described as the voice of Spirit) is stored in the *sahasrara* or seat of the soul in the cerebrum, and spreads thence into the body through the spinal astral river of life and its branches in the nervous system.

XX

Ah, my Beloved, fill the Cup that clears
TO-DAY of past Regrets and future Fears—
To-morrow?—Why, To-morrow I may be
Myself with Yesterday's Sev'n Thousand Years.

GLOSSARY—*Beloved:* The soul; God's image in man. ***The cup that clears:*** The blissful consciousness of the soul, which banishes all unhappiness. ***Past regrets:*** Sorrow over evil actions already performed, and their probable dire results. ***Future fears:*** Dread of repeating evil deeds under the influence of the law of habit, and of the evil that might impend from further misdeeds. ***Yesterday's sev'n thousand years:*** The infinite past, which embraces the numberless dead.

Spiritual Interpretation

O my Soul! fill my consciousness with the ambrosia of bliss, flowing from the cask of ecstasy. Naught but that divine communion can dispel the haunting memories of past errors and the fear of future wrongs, with their yield of evil consequences.

I dare not wait to find the all-freeing Cosmic Beloved! Tomorrow I may be with time's infinite yesterdays. Today with all my devotion I will intoxicate myself with the love of the Beloved. Today I will make Him my own.

Practical Application

We must fill this life that we love so dearly with the nectar of perpetual soul-peace. Otherwise we can never be free from the consciousness of long-past errors and the forebodings of future misfortunes.

Let us be happy now, today; then it matters not if we die tomorrow and join the procession in the corridors of the past, colonnaded with the countless years. For we shall carry with us priceless soul-treasures of peace, faith, and happiness to light our long journey toward the great Beloved.

XXI

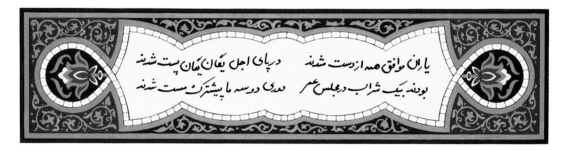

Lo! some we loved, the loveliest and the best
That Time and Fate of all their Vintage prest,
Have drunk their Cup a Round or two before,
And one by one crept silently to Rest.

GLOSSARY—***Time and fate:*** Death and karma (the law of cause and effect). ***Vintage prest:*** The wine of life pressed from the mortal body. ***Have drunk their cup a round or two before:*** Have died a short or a long while before us. ***To rest:*** To enjoy the peace of afterlife while awaiting a fresh mortal garment.

Spiritual Interpretation

Inevitably time, which brings all things to an end, and karma, its companion, stamp out in the press of death the precious wine of each human life. One by one—even the most beloved and lovely, those we have regarded as the flowers of souls—all must undergo this experience. Those who have already drunk their cup of death slip silently away, to rest undisturbed by mortal travail. Though the ordinary man looks upon death with dread and sadness, those who have gone before know it as a wondrous experience of peace and freedom.

Practical Application

This world is a stage where we are assembled to play our parts in individual, family, national, and international life. But at the summons of karmic law, we retire for a rest behind the earthly scene, awaiting assignment of our next role and of a new mortal costume in which to play it. We must not dwell sorrowfully on the time when the curtain will fall and our present role will be finished. Rather we should do our best to play our great or small part willingly and excellently, that we may deserve a welcome in the bosom of God. Otherwise, we will be forced by karma to return to this earth stage again and again until we perfect our part.

So, instead of letting time and fate rule our destiny, crushing out the vivacity of one incarnation after another, why not let God immortalize us with His celestial touch? No longer, then, will we need to creep into the lap of afterlife to rest. Being with God, we will be Eternal Life Itself, never again to be enslaved by limitations behind the prison walls of past, present, and future.

XXII

And we, that now make merry in the Room
They left, and Summer dresses in new Bloom,
*   Ourselves must we beneath the Couch of Earth*
Descend, ourselves to make a Couch — for whom?

GLOSSARY — ***Room:*** The earth, a stage for the drama of life. ***Summer dresses in new bloom:*** The summer of a new incarnation dresses our souls in fresh bodily garments. ***Beneath the couch of earth descend:*** The body must return to the earth elements whence

it came. ***For whom?*** A play on words, with two meanings: (1) We know not whose bones in future civilizations may sleep upon the couch our bones have made. (2) For whom, or what purpose, is this drama of life and death enacted?

Spiritual Interpretation

Life is ephemeral. Countless human actors have departed this earthly stage where we now make merry, unmindful of the time when our roles will end and our exit, too, will be demanded. Dressed for the summer of a new life in the rose blooms of fresh bodily costumes, we have come to disport ourselves in this earth-garden. But, as in so many lifetimes before, these new forms will have to return to the earth whence they came, destined to couch in future the discarded mortal garb of souls unknown to us, when they too shall be laid to rest on the abandoned robes in which we played our parts.

Practical Application

So long as we are on stage in the drama of life, we should play our part to the best of our ability. That is, we must try to understand the purpose of the drama, and why we have our particular role in it. We ought not to come here in ignorance life after life, only to depart still unconscious of life's meaning, as the animals do. Through God-communion, we must realize the mystery of life, grasp its whole meaning, so we will know why we and all other beings pass through these rounds of life and death. All too soon will come our turn to leave this world stage. Our bodies will be laid to sleep in the earth, and over them others will sleep in some far distant time. Such is the law of life. While we are enjoying this earth stage, with its enchanting scenery of natural beauty, let not the pursuit of short-lasting pleasures make us forget that happiness eternal is found in God, when in meditation we feel the lotus touch of His divine bliss.

XXIII

واندوه حال روزخارت گیرد   گلُزاره غصہ رحصارت گیرد

زان پیش کہ خاک درکنارت گیرد   ی خوربینا سبزہ وآب روان

Ah, make the most of what we yet may spend,
Before we too into the Dust descend;
Dust into Dust, and under Dust, to lie,
Sans Wine, sans Song, sans Singer, and — sans End.

GLOSSARY — *Make the most:* Seek the eternal, not the temporal. *Of what we yet may spend:* The time and conscious awareness still left to us in this life. *Into the dust descend:* Are snatched away by death. *Dust into dust:* The body made of earth commingles with the earth. *Under dust:* Our earthly remains will be covered by the dust of countless future generations, throughout aeons. *Sans wine, sans song, sans singer:* This mortal body will no more enjoy sense pleasures and human companions. *Sans end:* The mortal birth-and-death cycle of creation continues endlessly, as souls bound by the law of karma reincarnate in new bodies, life after life.

Spiritual Interpretation

Why end yet another incarnation with your true Self, the immortal soul, still identified with the delusion of mortal consciousness? Use wisely life's all too few remaining moments to free the soul's attention from short-lived sense joys to become engrossed in eternal ever-new Spirit Joy. At death this mortal body, which is formed of the earth and returns to dust, must relinquish its sense pleasures and companions. And they in their own turn will also lose their temporal forms and commingle with the dust of change. Thus continues endlessly the cycle of creation. No mortal can escape the karmic law — bondage to the effects of ego-initiated actions, which tie him to repeated births and deaths — unless he frees his soul through conscious God-realization.

Practical Application

The mortal body is itself naught but a clod of earth. It is the spirit within that creates in it a fertile garden of thoughts and actions. As human beings endowed with soul intelligence, it behooves us not to let mental weeds of unsavory habits take hold in the bodily soil. While the season for sowing is still unspent, we should use it for cultivating wholesome habits and worthwhile achievements. Let us not carelessly wait until all our pleasures, thoughts, inspirations—and our soul's ultimate desire for God-reunion—must commingle with the bodily dust in the oblivion of death. Let us harvest from those plants the fruits of God-realization and such heroic noble actions as will immortalize our memory when we are gone, and perpetually inspire others to seek God, the Divine Goal of our labors in the garden of life.

XXIV

قوی تفکر اند در مذہب و دین   جمعی متحیر اند در شک و یقین

ناگاه منادی برآید ز کمیـن   کای بیخبران راه نه آنست و نه این

Alike for those who for TO-DAY prepare,
And those that after a TO-MORROW stare,
*   A Muezzin from the Tower of Darkness cries*
"Fools! your Reward is neither Here nor There!"

GLOSSARY — *For today prepare:* Try to earn material happiness now. *After a tomorrow stare:* Expect future earthly solace. *A muezzin:* The voice of wisdom. *Tower of darkness:* The piled-up painful disillusionments of life from which we finally learn. *Your reward:* Lasting material happiness. *Neither here nor there:* Will not be found in the present nor the future.

Spiritual Interpretation

Foolish are those who singleheartedly concentrate on the pursuit of material happiness today, and those also who gaze longingly toward the dim promise of the future, waiting for the light of contentment to appear. The voice of wisdom calls to man from out of the dark despairs of repeated painful disillusionments, trying to remind him of his folly. Those who look for lasting happiness from material sources will never have real satisfaction, now or in the future.

Practical Application

To be steeped in materialism or to desire material contentment is to court disillusionment. From the many painful experiences of life that have shown us this, we should learn that material happiness deceives us. No matter how enjoyable the moment or how promising the future, material pleasure is temporal and fickle; its constant companion is disappointment and sorrow. This is because the soul can never feel satisfied with the foreign delusive happiness of the senses; it is always longing for its own forgotten joy of everlasting Spirit. Therefore it is foolish to waste time trying to get worthwhile results out of worthless activities. But from pursuits that are in harmony with our true soul nature, lasting, satisfying results will be forthcoming without any coaxing.

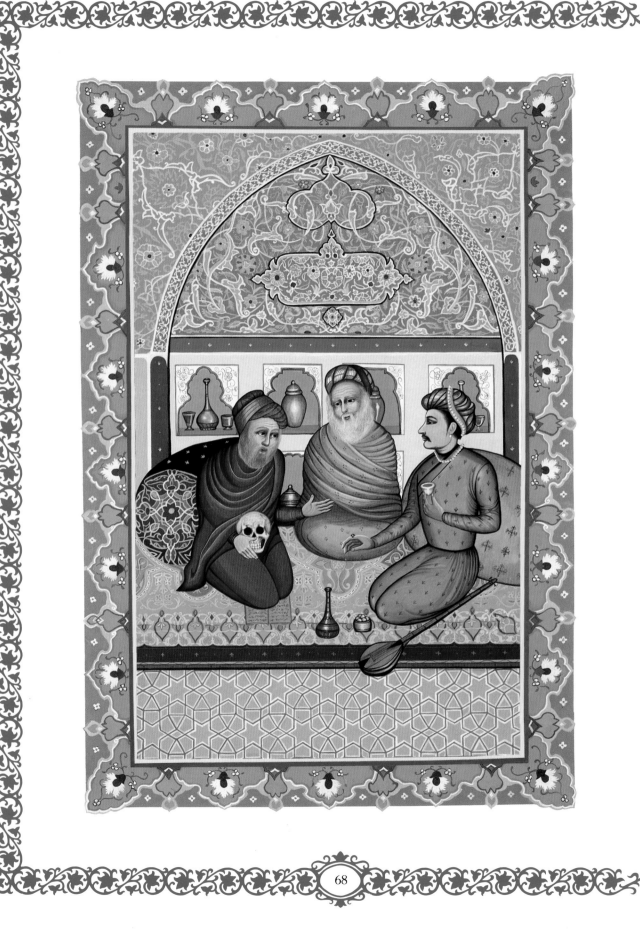

XXV

آنباكه زيش رنته انداى ساقى   دخاك غورخفته انداى ساقى

روباده خورو حقيت ازنى بشنو   بادست هرآنچه گفته انداى ساقى

Why, all the Saints and Sages who discuss'd
Of the Two Worlds so learnedly, are thrust
   Like foolish Prophets forth; their Words to Scorn
Are scatter'd, and their Mouths are stopt with Dust.

GLOSSARY — ***Two worlds:*** Here and the hereafter. ***Foolish prophets:*** Sages who are made to appear so, when they preach immortality and yet obey the laws of mortal existence. ***Words to scorn are scatter'd:*** Wisdom is mocked by the law of time and mortality. ***Mouths are stopt with dust:*** The voices of truth are silenced by death.

Spiritual Interpretation

Such is the mystery of the Lord's creation that even God-realized saints and savants, who discuss so knowingly and wisely the truths of this world and the hereafter, are spirited away by death like any ignorant man, as if they were mere prattling, self-elected prophets. All-conquering time and all-devouring death seem to be mocking their wise words, scattering them into the silent void. Their messages of fiery wisdom are muted; and the lips that once spoke so eloquently turn to dust, one with the dust of ancient tombs.

Practical Application

In this quatrain, Omar himself mocks the superficial view of the ordinary man, who is bewildered and doubtful because saints and sages possessed of great wisdom and God-realization have to succumb to death like anyone else. The truth is that even great savants have to obey the laws of God. They are not allowed to coerce disbelievers by performing miracles indiscriminately. Each human being must by his own effort awaken his soul's natural spiritual desire and faith, and work his own way to truth and to God. It is an insult to Spirit, and to the soul, to demand the physical presence of the great ones, and their miracles, as prerequisites to spiritual effort. The Lord takes His saints away to remind sincere souls that their belief and inspiration must not be conditioned by the earthly presence and personal counsel of the saints; that they themselves must experience truth, and hear from God's own lips the unravelling of the mystery of life and death.

So it is not the outward personalities but the inner lives of the saints that are worthy of our investigation. Even though they obey the laws of the physical universe and leave this earth simply, as do other men, their lives are extraordinary in the eyes of God. As He has revealed His utmost secrets to them, so will He reveal unto all true devotees the mysteries of His eternal kingdom.

XXVI

میفور که بزیر کل پس خواهی خفت
میبوس وبیامین و بی هم اوجفت
زنها ربکس مکعت و این راز نهفت
هر لاله پژمرده نخواهد بشگفت

Oh, come with old Khayyam, and leave the Wise
To talk; one thing is certain, that Life flies;
One thing is certain, and the Rest is Lies;
The Flower that once has blown for ever dies.

GLOSSARY — *Come with old Khayyam:* Experience the age-old truth of God-realization as discovered anew by Omar Khayyam. *Leave the wise to talk:* Forsake the theologians full of theories. *Life flies:* There is no time to waste. *One thing is certain:*

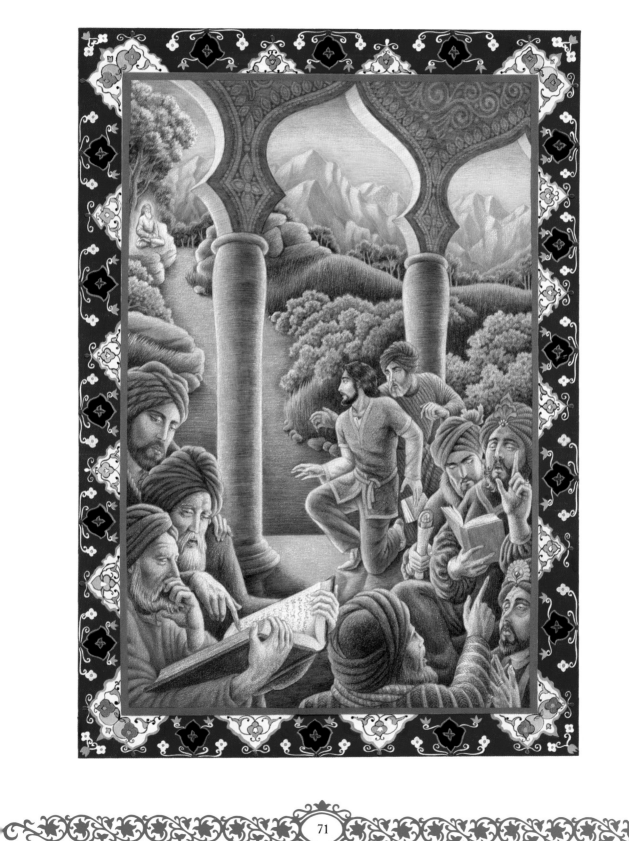

God alone is unchanging and everlasting. ***The rest is lies:*** The world of appearances is false. ***The flower that once has blown:*** The expression of life and of temporarily alluring temptation. ***For ever dies:*** Pleasures fade away after yielding momentary happiness; life is lost in the mystery of death.

Spiritual Interpretation

Oh, follow the ancient way of God-experience with Khayyam—who destroys decaying ignorance by communion with the divine *Aum* vibration* in meditation —and leave the theoretically wise to their theological discussions. Earthly life is fleeting; our short season should be used to seek God, the one unchangeable, ever-existing Certainty. On the oceanic bosom of Invisible Spirit, countless changing forms declare their reality, but they lie about their true nature. Creation is unreal and impermanent; Spirit alone is eternal and absolute, hidden beneath the deception of apparently real material phenomena.

Short-lived earthly pleasures that have bloomed in the garden of material consciousness, enthralling those who are ignorant of their real nature, soon lose their beauty and allure, and die. The marvelous flower of life itself ultimately fades and passes away, vanishing into the oblivion of infinity. Therefore seek in meditation the one Certainty; the hidden omnipresent God of Bliss.

Practical Application

Omar advises us: "Do not lose yourself by wandering in the trackless jungles of theology, or by tarrying in the gardens of false material pleasures that forever change and decay. Perceive by meditation what I myself have experienced and intuitionally tested: the divine bliss of God that lies within the soul. Waste not your time in intellectual discussions and paltry pleasures, for time is on the wing. In persevering meditation, try to contact the One Spirit, the only real Substance behind all appearances. Lift the veil of sensations, and in the secret soul-peace of daily silence find the positive proof of Divine Existence. Otherwise you will not know the ever-intensifying joy that can be felt as you go deep into the temple of quietness. The ever-increasing peace of meditation is the certain proof of the presence of that Bliss-God."

* God in His aspect of Creator; the Holy Ghost, the Amen, and the Word of the Bible; the creative voice of God: "In the beginning was the Word, and the Word was with God, and the Word was God" (John 1:1). *Aum* is heard in meditation and reveals to the devotee the Ultimate Truth.

XXVII

Myself when young did eagerly frequent
Doctor and Saint, and heard great Argument
About it and about: but evermore
Came out by the same Door as in I went.

GLOSSARY—*Myself when young:* To seek God during the period of youth is advantageous, as it imbues one's whole life with divine realization. *Doctor and saint:* Religious preceptors, or gurus, whose teachings and examples inspire seekers after God. *About it and about:* Concerning the theory of truth and the technique of realizing truth. *Came out by the same door as in I went:* In deep meditation I entered the door of intuitive Self-realization and experienced divine perceptions of truth. Through the same door I came out of my superconscious state into the conscious state, bringing those realizations to remain with me permanently.

(This stanza of the *Rubaiyat,* ordinarily interpreted as a sarcastic reference to the vanity of intellectual discussion on life's mysteries, is really a profound tribute to Khayyam's religious teachers, as proved by the first line of the next quatrain: "With them the seed of wisdom did I sow.")

Spiritual Interpretation

With the eagerness of youth, I frequented the haunts of saints and doctors of philosophy. In their quickening presence I entered the portals of awakened intuition, and listened with understanding to their subtle arguments about truth and the techniques of knowing truth. Responding enthusiastically, I applied my knowledge of the technique of God-contact in meditation, and the truths I had heard became my own intuitive divine perceptions. When I returned from the superconsciousness of God-communion to the conscious state, I brought those perceptions with me and established them as a part of my life. Thus, as I traveled back and forth through the door of intuitive Self-realization between the conscious and superconscious states, truth came to be an actual experience for me.

Practical Application

It is of good and lasting consequence if we eagerly cultivate true wisdom in the company of exalted teachers who have perceived truth. It is especially beneficial if we cultivate this wisdom early in life, so that it can be felt throughout all the years of our existence. By listening to the truth-exuding discussions of God-knowing souls, and applying the technique of God-contact they give us, it is easy to reach God through the door of Self-realization. In the peace of meditation, we can enter that door and go into the sanctuary of bliss; and when we come out of deep, joyous meditation, we can bring peace and joy with us and establish them permanently in all the rooms of our life. Every divine truth we experience in superconsciousness we can continue to feel in our intuition during the ordinary conscious state of daily life and activity.

XXVIII

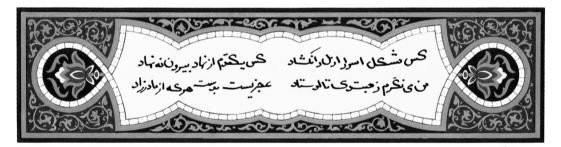

With them the Seed of Wisdom did I sow,
And with my own hand labour'd it to grow:
And this was all the Harvest that I reap'd —
"I came like Water, and like Wind I go."

GLOSSARY— ***With them:*** In the company of wise doctors and saints who taught me (referred to in the previous quatrain). ***Seed of wisdom:*** The teachings and contact of

the gurus or religious teachers who instilled in me the desire for realization of truth. ***Did I sow:*** I implanted that wisdom in the soil of my soul. ***With my own hand labour'd it to grow:*** My sincere efforts in daily meditation nurtured the growth of my realization. ***All the harvest:*** Self-realization. ***I came like water:*** When I began my search for God, I was weak and unstable, like water. ***Like wind I go:*** I became etherealized, powerful and free; my astralized and super-refined spirit became omnipresent—spread in all directions, like the wind.

Spiritual Interpretation

"From Self-realized masters I procured the seed of wisdom, and sowed it in the garden of my mind, which I had ploughed into deep furrows of devotion. Regularly I sprinkled the wisdom-seed with the waters of deep concentration in the silence of meditation, that it might grow and bear the ever-fragrant fiery flower of immortality. At last I reaped the divine harvest, vaster beyond imagining of all my expectations for the little spiritual effort I had made.

"My mind had been a river of material desire flowing through the tracts of matter. Now the divine sun-warmth of the soul, emerging from behind the clouds of ignorance, has evaporated the materialistic waters of my life and changed it into a mighty wind of soul-power spreading over the bosom of God's omnipresence."

Practical Application

The seed of wisdom is given by the guru or master of Self-realization; but the soil, or receptivity, and the cultivation of that seed must be supplied by the devotee.

Following the example of the masters, we should sow the seed of wisdom in the soil of our consciousness, and make earnest efforts to nurture it with the waters of self-discipline and daily meditation. Self-discipline is not self-torture; it is the way to organize and concentrate the unruly forces of the mind on those specific habits of living that can bring us true happiness. By doggedly following the methods of self-discipline we can rid ourselves of restlessness, bad habits, and misery-producing desires, and become truly happy. When we are weak, restless, and mentally unstable, we remain earthbound, like water. But when we become spiritualized by self-discipline and deep meditation, we soar like the wind in the omnipresence of our true soul nature.

At first, devotees search for God like restless rivers, still rippling with many earth-bound desires. But in time, when we have overcome those desires, God changes us into Spirit; then our souls and our understanding float in all directions of Blissful Omnipresence.

XXIX

آورده بامضطرام اول بوجود جز حیرتم از حیات چیزی نفزود
رفتیم باکراه و ندانیم چه بود زین آمدن و بودن زین رفتن مقصود

Into this Universe, and why not knowing,
Nor whence, like Water willy-nilly flowing;
And out of it, as Wind along the Waste,
I know not whither, willy-nilly blowing.

GLOSSARY—*Into this universe:* Born on earth in its cosmic environment. *Not knowing:* In a state of ignorance at first, I knew not the reason for this mortal existence. *Nor whence:* Nor the origin of being. *Willy-nilly flowing:* Coming helplessly to this earth. *Out of it:* Free of mortal limitations. *As wind:* Like Spirit. *Along the waste:* Soaring above matter. *I know not whither:* I know not the boundaries of the infinite sphere of Eternity.

Spiritual Interpretation

"I knew not the reason why I came into this universe; neither did I know, until now, from what Invisible Source the water of my life came helplessly flowing, losing itself in aimless wanderings on the tracts of earth. I am earthbound no more; like a mighty wind my soul springs free, spreading everywhere in the sphere of Spirit, whose infinite boundaries I know not nor comprehend. By divine ecstasy my gross life has been changed into Eternal Life."

Practical Application

Most souls come helplessly and unthinkingly to earth without knowing the reason why. To overcome our ignorance, we must progressively develop ourselves to the best of our ability and knowledge. By drawing inspiration from the lives of great men, we shall rise above all narrow confinements of habit-bound thought and custom into the firmament of free thought and universal understanding. And by contacting ever-new Joy on the altar of meditation, we shall lose all grossness and feel the Omnipresent Spirit. With utter surrender to the will of the Lord, our souls will ever expand like a sphere of bliss in the boundless kingdoms of Omnipresence.

XXX

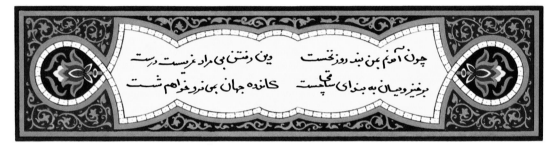

What, without asking, hither hurried whence?
And, without asking, whither hurried hence!
Another and another Cup to drown
The Memory of this Impertinence!

GLOSSARY — *Without asking:* Without our conscious permission. ***Hither hurried whence:*** Sent to earth from what unknown place. ***Whither hurried hence:*** To what strange land are we spirited away from this earth? ***Another and another cup:*** Repeated experiences of divine consciousness through intuition. ***Drown the memory of this impertinence:*** Banish the memory of past ignorant thinking, the mortal consciousness that is an insult to our immortal, God-knowing soul nature.

Spiritual Interpretation

It appears that, unconsulted, we are hurried here to earth from an unknown sphere; and then, without any solicitation on our part, we are hastily spirited away to a strange land. Living in a state of ignorance, most human beings do not understand that through the will of God they originally came on earth to be entertained; and would soon have gone back to Him if they had not developed mortal desires here.

Their hurried entry and exit on earth in utter ignorance and unknowing, incarnation after incarnation, is due to their forsaking inner God-consciousness and embracing outer sense-consciousness, which binds their souls to the ever-revolving wheel of karma: the law of cause and effect governing all mortals.

Now let us drink another and another cup of intuitional inspiration, until we have drowned mortal consciousness: the impertinent memory of having been the terror-stricken pawns of a destiny that insultingly brought us back and forth in ignorance—the memory that audaciously keeps invading our consciousness against our command.

Practical Application

Seemingly from nowhere, we have been brought and jailed like prisoners behind the bars of mortal limitations; and as suddenly we are freed and sent away into the womb of mystery. There is no use in bemoaning what must inevitably happen to all who live and die in mortal consciousness. It is best to dissolve all constantly upcropping, unwelcome pessimisms by repeatedly becoming intoxicated with the ever-new Joy of daily meditation. The deeper we go into that Joy—which is God—the more we shall realize our divine soul-nature, and thus regain our immortal freedom.

XXXI

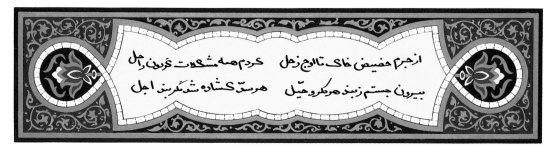

Up from Earth's Centre through the Seventh Gate
I rose, and on the Throne of Saturn sate,
And many Knots unravel'd by the Road;
But not the Knot of Human Death and Fate.

GLOSSARY—*Earth's centre:* Defined in Yoga treatises as the *Muladhara chakra*, located in the coccygeal plexus; the first or lowest spiritual center in the spine. It is the

first gate through which the interiorized consciousness and life have to pass in their upward climb to Spirit in the brain. *The seventh gate:* The *Sahasrara*, highest yogic center of divine consciousness and concentrated life force, located in the brain at the top of the head. This center is figuratively spoken of in Yoga as the thousand-petaled lotus, because the concentrated power of Spirit enthroned here emanates thousands of rays of divine light. *I rose:* I lifted my consciousness and life through the six cerebrospinal *chakras* to the thousand-petaled lotus. *On the throne of Saturn sate:* The "throne" refers to the seat of consciousness and life in man, concentrated in the brain and the subcenters in the spine. "Saturn" here refers to Satan, the negative aspect of the cosmic creative force, which keeps all creation in a state of delusion, or seeming separation from God, through the power of *maya*, ignorance. The ordinary man is ruled by this ignorance. But in the state of uplifted divine consciousness, ignorance is dethroned and wisdom rules in its stead. *Many knots unravel'd by the road:* My consciousness passed through all seven cerebrospinal centers, untying in each one the knots of life and consciousness that had bound the soul to the body. Many cosmic mysteries were revealed with the opening of each center. *Not the knot of human death and fate:* The soul is not permanently free from karma (the effects of one's past actions or so-called fate), or from death, until it has fully overcome delusion and leaves its physical-, astral-, and causal-body encasements and merges in Spirit.

Spiritual Interpretation

"In deep meditation, I transcended the sensory perceptions of the body and experienced divine realization by lifting my life force and consciousness upward through the yoga *chakras* (the spiritual cerebrospinal centers), from the earth vibration in the coccyx* to the thousand-petaled lotus in the brain. King Ignorance, who sat on the throne of consciousness and ruled my life in the body-identified state, was deposed; and I, the all-wise soul, one with Spirit, reigned in his stead.

"Ascending the spinal highway, I had unraveled in each of the six lower *chakras* the knots of life and consciousness that had tied me to the body. Thus, when I en-

---

* In defining the many components of cosmic creation, Yoga treatises refer to five elements: earth, water, fire, air, and ether. These are not physical in nature; they are five creative vibratory forces into which the cosmic creative vibration (*Aum* or Amen), the ultimate building-block of all creation, differentiates itself to construct and maintain the universe and man's body. In the human form, these five elements create and sustain the body and all its functions, operating in and through the five lower spinal *chakras:* Earth, coccygeal center *(Muladhara);* Water, sacral center *(Svadhishthana);* Fire, lumbar center *(Manipura);* Air, dorsal center *(Anahata);* Ether, cervical center *(Vishuddha).*

tered the seventh center, the thousand-petaled lotus, I was momentarily free in cosmic consciousness.

"But this experience in meditation did not completely liberate me. Because of my karma, the results of my past actions, I could not escape permanently into Spirit. To sunder karmic bonds and conquer death forever, I had first to learn by deeper meditation to consciously go in and out of the body at will. This mastery, and the wisdom of divine consciousness it brings, frees the soul permanently from delusion. Then the soul can leave not only the physical body, but the astral and causal encasements* as well, and merge in Omnipresent Spirit—a fully liberated soul!"

The ordinary man's consciousness in the wakeful state is centered on the palate and other regions of the flesh where he experiences the sensations of taste, sound, smell, sight, and touch; hence he is conscious of the body. In sleep, man's mind and life force retire from the outer flesh to the region of the heart and the lower spine. His attention is thus disconnected from the disturbance of sensory perceptions; in deep sleep his mind is filled with peace. He is subconsciously aware of being near the invisible, blissful, formless sphere of the soul.

By deep meditation, the mind and life force can be transferred not only from the senses, but also from the internal organs, and lifted up the spine—through the earth center in the coccyx, and the other spiritual centers in the spine—to the brain. These cerebrospinal centers are the gates through which life force and consciousness flow outwardly to the flesh and inwardly to Spirit. The nerves and muscles are the roads along which life force and consciousness travel outward from these centers toward the senses and material enjoyment. But when the life force and consciousness travel inward, back through the nervous system and through the spine—the only road to divine consciousness—the cerebrospinal gates open upward, untying the knots in those centers that bind the soul to body and matter consciousness.

The seven gates through which the soul prisoner has to escape into Omnipresence are the coccygeal, sacral, lumbar, dorsal, and cervical centers in the spine; the medullary center, interrelated with the Christ center in the forehead; and the thousand-petaled lotus. These seven spiritual centers are spoken of as *chakras* or lotuses in the

---

* As a man may wear undergarments, a suit, and an overcoat, so the incarnate soul has three coverings. The innermost garment is the causal or ideational body, whose essence is the fine vibration of thought, God-thought. The composition of the causal body is thirty-five ideas of Spirit, from which come the grosser manifestations of the nineteen elements composing the astral body and the sixteen basic chemical elements of the physical body. (See footnote on page 51.)

Yoga scriptures of India, and as "the mystery of the seven stars" and the "seven churches" in the Christian Bible (Revelation 1:20).

The cranial and spinal centers of consciousness in ordinary beings are cloaked by satanic ignorance, or *maya*, and reveal only the outer world of matter and the senses. Omar Khayyam's use of the name "Saturn" for satanic ignorance is apt: the Saturnalia, ancient Roman festival of Saturn, has come to symbolize abandonment to sense pleasures. To attain divine consciousness, it is necessary to dislodge this satanic ignorance by establishing meditation-nurtured wisdom in the cerebrospinal centers and inner consciousness. In deep meditation, when the soul arrives at the thousand-rayed Throne of Light in the cranium, it dethrones King Ignorance and drives his ruling ministers from all the lower centers.

But even though the devotee arrives at this high state in meditation, he still does not learn the final mystery of life and death; nor does he get away from the influence of his karma—the effects of prenatal seeds of actions sown in other incarnations, and of new seeds of actions in this life. When the evil effect of a forgotten, previously initiated cause suddenly pounces on us, we speak of the event as fate. In the light of wisdom, we can see that so-called fateful happenings are usually brought about by unremembered actions of the past, in this life or in previous incarnations. Every cause has an effect: good actions produce good effects; wrong actions, bad effects. So long as the soul is a prisoner of karma, it is subject to the recurrent cycles of birth and death.

To learn the final mystery of life and death, and to be free forever from the imperatives of karma, the yogi must be able to take his soul out of the body through the seven cerebrospinal gates into the presence of the almighty, all-pervading Spirit, and return—consciously, any time, at will. By this highest wisdom he learns to destroy the delusion of being imprisoned in the three bodies—causal, astral, and physical. He may then consciously cast off these bodies and merge in Spirit, a free soul. Only then is the mystery of life and death and "fate" finally solved: the soul is no longer under the cosmic compulsion of these experiences, which are integral to the mayic realm of creation.

If salt water is encased in a sealed jar and enclosed in two other consecutively sealed jars, and immersed in the ocean, the imprisoned brine in the innermost jar cannot mingle with the vast ocean waters, even if one outer jar is broken. So also the soul of man, confined in three bodies, moves in the ocean of Spirit. At death only the physical body is discarded; the soul, still imprisoned in the two other bodies, is not free to unite with Spirit. By wisdom, the soul after death can come out of the astral and causal confinements as well, and become Spirit, as the salt water commingles with the ocean when all three jars are broken.

After death, Jesus did not arise for three days. This period was the time required to work out the karma of the three bodies—karma he had taken on himself to relieve the suffering of his disciples and the world—and lift the soul above the enclosures of the astral and causal bodies. Even divine souls, though inwardly free, obey outwardly the laws of the cosmos. Without willingly accepting a certain amount of cosmic delusion, they could not remain incarnate in this world of *maya*. The very atoms of their bodies would dissolve in Spirit.

Practical Application

The ordinary man thinks that praying to God is all that is necessary to know Him. But blind, absentminded prayers of years remain unanswered, as is clearly shown by the difference between the lives of theoretical theologians and God-saturated sages. Inventions come, not through blind prayers, but by scientific application of the mind and of universal laws. Similarly, the greatest of all coveted discoveries—Self-realization—can be made by applying the scientific art of freeing the enslaved consciousness from the bondage of restlessness and consciously uniting it with God.

Yoga, as discovered by the master minds of India, teaches the art of scientifically uniting the individualized soul with omnipresent Spirit. A yogi is one who, through psychophysical self-control and meditation, consciously takes his mind from the sense-conscious state, and from the subconscious sleep state, into the supremely joyous superconscious, Christ-conscious, and cosmic-conscious states of Spirit.

While the yogi transfers his mind from the sense-conscious and subconscious states to the superconscious state, he simultaneously experiences certain physical transitions in the location of his mind: from the objects of the physical senses to the spinal centers, and finally to the highest center in the brain. In the conscious state the body and the world are perceived. In the subconscious state the mind and life travel through the grotto of the lower physical spinal plexuses; the yogi experiences dreams or deep peace. In the superconscious state the yogi's consciousness goes through the spiritual centers in the spinal canal and medulla and he realizes his true soul nature. In the

Christ-conscious state, the soul attains the universal consciousness of Spirit, oneness with every particle in creation. In the cosmic-conscious state, the soul merges with the omnipresence of Spirit, not only within, but also beyond all creation.

Omar Khayyam says that these spiritual experiences, which came to him, are available to all who scientifically unite themselves with God. By attaining these different states of consciousness in deep meditation, everyone can unravel the ultimate mystery of life and death.

This quatrain in the *Rubaiyat* clearly shows Omar Khayyam's advancement on the path of yoga — not of wine!

XXXII

There was a Door to which I found no Key:
There was a Veil past which I could not see:
Some little Talk awhile of ME and THEE
There seem'd — and then no more of THEE and ME.

GLOSSARY — **Door:** The portal between the finite and the Infinite; the manifested and the Absolute; the soul and Spirit. **I found no key:** I could not enter. **Veil:** The finer perceptions of divine states of consciousness that yet hid the Unmanifested Absolute. **Some little talk awhile of me and Thee:** The perception of separation between soul and Spirit, due to the law of relativity. **No more of Thee and me:** In union with the Absolute, no separate existence is felt between the devotee and the great Cosmic Deity.

Spiritual Interpretation

"After I had withdrawn my consciousness and life force, switching off the lamps of the muscles, senses, heart, and the cerebrospinal *chakras*, my soul perception reached the seventh center, the thousand-petaled lotus in the cerebral region. I stood at the door of Infinity, unable to find the key to its mysteries, the way to complete freedom in Spirit beyond the physical-, astral-, and causal-body encasements. My soul, reaching even this high state of attainment, could not penetrate the veil of the inner light of superconsciousness, Christ consciousness, and cosmic consciousness, beyond which lay the *sanctum sanctorum*, the holy of holies, the abode of the Unmanifested Beloved—the Absolute.

"There was a little 'talk' or conscious intuitional vibratory exchange between soul (me) and Spirit (Thee); and then, in deeper ecstasy, I became united with the indescribable Infinite. In that oneness with the Absolute, there remained no separate existence of my individual soul. 'A tiny bubble of laughter, I am become the Sea of Mirth Itself.' "*

In the progressive states of spiritual awakening, the first experience is superconsciousness, the realization of the Self as soul, individualized Spirit. In deeper ecstasy, the consciousness enters Christ consciousness, oneness with the consciousness of God that is manifested in all creation—every atom is realized as a part of one's own being. In a still higher state, the soul attains cosmic consciousness, realization of God as the Supreme Creator from whom all differentiated forms and states of consciousness devolve. All these are seen to be of the same essence of this one Divine Being.

In oneness with God in cosmic consciousness, there is first an element of separation—"Some little talk awhile of me and Thee"—the individualized Self realizing its oneness with the Supreme Self, yet experiencing God, the Creator, as though apart from Him. Communion with God, or the experience of God, presupposes duality: the knower and the Known. We cannot experience or commune with the Absolute, which is beyond all differentiation. To know the Absolute, we must merge with the Unmanifested Spirit. In this oneness, there is "then no more of Thee and me"—only the One, who is infinite, ever-existing, ever-conscious, ever-new Bliss. Of this state of oneness, the Hindu scriptures say: "He who knows, he knows; naught else knows."

Practical Application

In the expansion of human love into divine love we find a corollary to the metaphysical experience of oneness just described. Two selfish souls united in matrimony remain apart in spirit, each hedged in by self-love and egoism. Though outwardly

* From Paramahansa Yogananda's poem "Samadhi," in his *Autobiography of a Yogi*, Chapter 14.

united, such souls never find the key to celestial union, and are unable to look beyond the veil of human love, which is subject to constant change and death through the law of relativity. But if two souls realize the follies of self-love and relinquish selfishness and blind inharmony, then their love changes into divine love. They find that in the beginning, a wall of selfishness divided them as "thee" and "me." But later, with the growth of their understanding of the true nature of love, the wall of separation between these two awakened souls dissolves, and their love becomes the love of God. In that love they know true union, or oneness.

No human love can be complete or perfect without God's love. No marriage can be lasting or truly fruitful without the catalyst of divine love. No love is real love until it is one with God's love; for all true love comes from God alone. Human love, to be divine, must be deep and selfless. Purify the heart's love until it becomes divine.

When, after many incarnations of trials and disappointments in human relationships, two souls are united in divine love, they do not realize at first that they have found the key to the ultimate mysteries and nature of love—their vision cannot fathom the depth of divine love, which has its source in God. In this state, these two souls blissfully enjoy their relationship with one another in the feeling of unconditional, selfless love. Then, after a while, they fall into the ecstasy of oneness in God's love, and lose entirely the consciousness of separate existence. This is the law of divine love through which Spirit is ever seeking to draw back the many into the One. When a human relationship is perfected by a oneness with God's love, its diversity merges in harmony with the eternal One.

The perfecting of love can be achieved between two souls in such relationships as lover and beloved, parent and child, friend and friend, or the highest, guru and disciple. When two souls transmute pure human love into divine love and become one in God's love, they are able to give His divine love equally to all, and thus help to draw other souls into unity with the One.

XXXIII

در گوش دلم لغت قلم پنهانی   جلسی که تضا بود زین میدان

در گردش خزش آمد در اوست بری   خودرا برهانذمی زسر گردانی

Then to the rolling Heav'n itself I cried,
Asking, "What Lamp had Destiny to guide
Her little Children stumbling in the Dark?"
And—"A blind Understanding!" Heav'n replied.

GLOSSARY—***Rolling heav'n:*** Unfolding heavenly blissful consciousness felt in deep meditation. ***I cried:*** I questioned Omniscience, the all-pervading Spirit. ***What lamp:*** What kind of intelligence. ***Destiny:*** Law of cause and effect, or karma, which operates with a just and mathematical exactitude. "Whatsoever a man soweth, that shall he also reap."* ***Little children stumbling in the dark:*** Human beings who err because of lack of wisdom, and consequently fall victim to self-created bad habits and karmic effects of wrong actions. ***A blind understanding:*** The imperfect understanding of mortal intelligence, worldly wise but spiritually blind.

Spiritual Interpretation

"As my soul delved into the truth-revealing vibratory heavenly sphere of ecstasy, I compared my joyous emancipated state with that of God's other human children who are stumbling in ignorance and misery, led by their individual self-created destiny of bad habits and karma (effects of their actions); and I asked the heavenly-state-pervading Spirit: 'What guided them to their error and doom?'

"The Inner Voice replied: 'A worldly-wise, materially keen intelligence, which, being spiritually blind, is thus devoid of all-seeing, all-wise intuition.'"

* Galatians 6:7.

Practical Application

It is difficult even for great wise men to know always what is truth. How much harder it is, then, for human beings who have limited intelligence to follow the right pathways in life. Their decisions are often impulsive reactions to sensory attractions, or are unthinking responses to habits and other self-created karmic circumstances in their lives. The only lamp that lights their way is their innate but imperfect instinctive understanding, which is partly intelligent, and partly blind. Being thus limited, this instinctive understanding may wrongly lead God's children to stumble into the pits of delusion. Those who are constantly stumbling show us how very poorly guided we can be by this blind instinctive understanding.

All of God's children are endowed with the highest intelligence: intuition, the all-knowing wisdom of the soul. But so long as one's intuition remains undeveloped, he is guided mainly by the limited understanding of mortal intelligence, with only occasional promptings of intuitive wisdom. Thus he engages in some good actions, but also in many wrong actions, and acquires many bad habits. Through the operation of the law of cause and effect, or karma, he finds himself following helplessly his own self-created destiny, which often leads to misery. But from the consequences of his wrong actions and the rewarding effects of his good actions, his understanding grows. His innate intuition gradually awakens and begins to guide him with wisdom. He is led from misery to happiness, from religious superstition to the realization of truth, from dark ignorance to the joyous, emancipated state of divine ecstasy.

XXXIV

Then to this earthen Bowl did I adjourn
My Lip the secret Well of Life to learn:
*   And Lip to Lip it murmur'd—"While you live*
Drink!—for once dead you never shall return."

GLOSSARY—***Then:*** After feeling the vast Spirit without creation. ***This earthen bowl:*** The physical body with its earthly consciousness. ***My lip:*** My individual wisdom. ***The secret Well of Life to learn:*** To feel the hidden waters of Spirit trickling through all material life. ***Lip to lip it murmur'd:*** The transcendental Spirit intimated to my inner wisdom. ***While you live:*** So long as you have Self-realization in this present incarnation. ***Drink:*** Feel the divine bliss of Spirit within you and all things. ***Once dead:*** Once in that state wherein your soul is completely free, not only from the confinement of the physical body of sixteen elements (as in death), but also from the astral and causal bodies.* ***Never shall return:*** Will not be forced anymore by the law of cause and effect to reincarnate.

Spiritual Interpretation

After feeling in *samadhi* meditation the vast Spirit in all space, without body consciousness, my soul returned to the brittle earthly bowl of flesh. There also, by

---

* The astral body is made of conscious electricity or luminous life force. The causal body, which contains the residual seeds of actions or stored-up tendencies for future lives, is made of thirty-five ideas of Spirit from which come the grosser manifestations of the astral and physical bodies. The man of realization knows how to free his soul which is made in God's image—not only from the bondage of the physical body, but the astral and causal bodies as well, and to unite it with omnipresent Spirit.

divinely awakened wisdom, I tasted the waters of Bliss, which, trickling down from the well of Eternal Life, reside in the body and flow through all life. This blissful Cosmic Consciousness intimated through my intuitive realization: "Drink unceasingly of Spirit in waking consciousness as well as in meditation, and your soul shall be freed forever from enforced cycles of birth and death."

The devotee in the first state of ecstatic God-contact *(sabikalpa samadhi)* sees and feels Spirit as formless, all-pervading, ever-new Bliss, without any perception of creation. The devotee is not unconscious, but so engrossed in God-consciousness that he is oblivious of cosmic creation. He sees the ocean of Spirit without the waves of manifested forms.

Later, by higher ecstatic divine communion *(nirbikalpa samadhi)*, the devotee learns to bring back with him to the conscious state his experience of God-contact, and to keep it constantly united to body perception. The ordinary human being is conscious of his body as belonging to an ego; but the devotee in the *nirbikalpa* state is conscious of his body as God-possessed. In this highest experience of Cosmic Consciousness, the devotee, like God, is simultaneously conscious of Spirit, all matter, and his little body, too—he beholds the Ocean of Spirit with all Its waves of creation. He intuitively feels in his bodily "bowl" the Well of eternal Life. Cosmic Consciousness signifies to him: "O devotee, so long as you are consciously alive with Self-realization, drink the immortal nectar of Spirit! For once you have become metaphysically dead—able at will to get out of the confinement of the three bodies (physical, astral, and causal)—you will never again have to reincarnate on this doleful earth, forced to return here by the law of cause and effect (karma) that governs all lives."

Practical Application

An attitude of impractical otherworldliness won't do so long as we are incarnate on this earthly plane. No matter how high we soar in the skies of transcendental wisdom and intellectuality, engrossed in ultimate truths and the highest ideals and concepts, at the same time we ought to keep our feet on the earth, by being able to drink the beauty and goodness honeycombed in all life. The truly wise know how to apply their lofty concepts and experiences to the relativities of day-to-day existence, and thereby bring out the best from all circumstances.

A man without knowledge of reincarnation thinks he lives and dies only once, and will never return to earth; thus he feels he ought to make the most of his days by seeking as much material pleasure as possible. Such persons reason that whether we are wise or ignorant, we will all lose our mortal life just the same—and cannot return even if we want to—so what is the use of worry and struggle, and of scientific effort to learn the laws of life? But a desultory materialistic life is a miserable existence. We should therefore remember that it is advantageous for the immediate present—as well as for the effect it will have on our future—to live our life in the safe castle of wisdom rather than on the edge of the misery-erupting, scorching volcano of spiritual pessimism and bad habits.

Whether one believes in reincarnation or not, it is true that each soul is born on earth *in a particular form* only once. Hence, everyone should play his present part well while in this divine earthly drama. He should do his very best by properly utilizing his chance of this one particular lifetime to fulfill successfully his divinely ordained role, and thus please the Heavenly Father and assure his own permanent happiness.

XXXV

I think the Vessel, that with fugitive
Articulation answer'd, once did live,
*   And merry-make; and the cold Lip I kiss'd*
How many Kisses might it take – and give!

GLOSSARY—*Vessel:* The physical body, with its body-consciousness. *Fugitive articulation:* The voice that has "escaped" the limitation of physical expression to articulate in the universal language of thought vibrations understood by the intuition. *Answer'd:* Body-consciousness responded to the queries put to it by the intuition of the soul. *Once did live, and merry-make:* While in the waking state, the consciousness was sometimes attracted to the God-joy within, and sometimes to the frivolities of the senses. *Cold lip:* The deathlike state of the body in ecstasy; also, the deathlike negative state of the soul when it manifests as body-consciousness. *How many kisses might it take— and give:* The latent power of the body or material consciousness to receive and respond to divine realization.

Spiritual Interpretation

"In *samadhi* meditation I, the soul, beheld the body-vessel in a state of suspended animation, outwardly deathlike (or deep sleeplike) in its trance of ecstasy, but inwardly awake. In divine introspection I conversed with the inwardly tuned body-consciousness, and it responded to the critical queries of my soul, articulating in the universal, intuitively understood language of thought vibrations. Expressing itself freely about its mortal life-experiences, the body-consciousness confided how at times it lived the godly life as a true image of Spirit, rejoicing in the God-joy within; but how at other times it preferred a worldly life, reveling in the trivial merry-making pleasures of the flesh.

"My soul 'kissed,' or tried to instill its divine perceptions in, my matter-loving body, which lacked the warmth of wisdom to keep it spiritually alive. I wanted to see if the body-consciousness would respond and become immortally spiritualized by exchanging its worldly-pleasure perceptions for perceptions of the divine love and joy of my soul, through repeated experiences of ecstasy."

In *samadhi*, the body has the outward appearance of deep sleep; all physiological functions are in a state of suspended animation. The soul, though absent from the physical body-vessel, remains inwardly spiritually alive, intoxicated with God-joy. Just as in sleep the body is partially inert but the mind is happy, so in the trancelike state of ecstasy, a deeper state of conscious sleep, the body is totally immobile, but the soul is inwardly awake and superbly happy.* As it would be foolish to be alarmed at the thought of going to sleep, so is it foolish to fear the experience of going into the ecstatic trance of *samadhi*.

When a man reading a book with deep concentration fails to hear a sound, he is not said to be unconscious. He is so engrossed in the book that he is outwardly oblivious to all sensations. Likewise, the adept can so inwardly merge himself in the joyous contact of divine consciousness that he is not cognizant of his bodily sensations or outward surroundings.

Ecstasy, or divine trance, is not a mental chloroform producing inner and outer unconsciousness. A person who is unconscious both inwardly and outwardly is in a state of catalepsy; this can be induced by illness, or by pressure on certain glands — a technique employed by some so-called yogis. But the trance of true *samadhi* is produced only by the extreme intoxication of Divine Love.

In ecstasy, when the body is in a deathlike or deep sleeplike state, the inwardly tuned body-consciousness is able to receive perceptions of Divine Love from the pure consciousness of the soul. This experience, when oft repeated, will help the body to forget its delusive attachment to material pleasures and become spiritually alive. To live only on the pleasure-plane of the senses is to be truly dead. To be awake in God

* Mystics of all religions have been observed in the breathless and motionless trance of *samadhi*. Among these may be mentioned St. Teresa of Avila, whose body would become so immovably fixed that the astonished nuns in the convent were unable to alter her position or to rouse her to outward consciousness.

and withdrawn from the outer world is to be really alive, for this is the true state of the Self, the soul.

Those who at will can reach complete absorption in prayer, or who practice a scientific yoga technique for attaining interiorization, can ultimately reach *sabikalpa samadhi*, in which the consciousness is with God but the body is in a trancelike state. Only a very few can attain, while on this earth plane, the highest ecstasy of *nirbikalpa samadhi*. In this state, the consciousness remains in unbroken communion with God while outwardly it continues to perform through the body, accomplishing its material duties with extraordinary efficiency but in a divinely nonattached manner. Those who can reach *nirbikalpa samadhi* find soul liberation in God in this life.

Practical Application

No matter how spiritually dead a person is outwardly, in his soul within he is still a powerful image of God. By delving in short-lived material pleasures, the outgoing expression of the soul temporarily assumes a negative nature, or ego, in which it feels identified with the body, and forgets the superior rejoicings of God-contact within. It is our duty to inspire courage in our souls, which have shrouded their true nature with ignorant living, and to try to awaken a spiritual response in them. By riotous sensual living, all the candles of happiness are consumed at once. By self-controlled, wisdom-guided living, the lamps of the ever new joy of God burn brightly forever on the altar of the soul's immortality.

XXXVI

For in the Market-place, one Dusk of Day,
I watch'd the Potter thumping his wet Clay:
And with its all obliterated Tongue
It murmur'd – "Gently, Brother, gently, pray!"

GLOSSARY—*Market-place:* The sphere of Cosmic Vibration whence come all created beings. *One dusk of day:* The state of ecstasy, when the sun of consciousness sets on body-awareness and shines with God-consciousness. *I watched the Potter:* I beheld with my inner all-seeing spiritual eye the Cosmic Creative Intelligence. *Thumping his wet clay:* Transforming cosmic energy into human forms. *Its all obliterated tongue:* The silent intuitive intelligence of the reincarnating soul. *"Gently, Brother, gently, pray":* "O Cosmic Law, please relax your exacting rule of justice when applying it to my life."

Spiritual Interpretation

During ecstasy—when the sun of my consciousness had set on body-awareness, and, sinking into Spirit, was aglow with God-consciousness—I stood in the sphere of Cosmic Vibration, in which all created beings have their origin. I beheld with my spiritual eye the divine Creative Intelligence condensing cosmic energy into atoms, and molding them into embryonic bodies to serve as dwelling places for reincarnating souls.

The silent intuitive intelligence of these souls—who were compelled by karma to take rebirth in the imprisoning limitations of flesh—prayed to the Cosmic Law, with which the Creative Intelligence cooperates in shaping new bodies for new incarnations: "Be gentle, regardless of what I deserve, and temper your unrelenting justice when determining the karmic effects to be reaped from my past-life wrong actions."

Practical Application

No matter how engrossed we are with our creative work in the busy atmosphere of the marketplace of this world, we should go into the silence of deep meditation in the twilight of the early morning and at the day's end when our duties are done. Communion with God will enable us to feel the workings of the Divine Intelligence as the true Creator of all things. That Intelligence, influenced by the Cosmic Law, is the hand of God at work in creation. But we must remember that to a great extent it is we, by our free-will-initiated actions, who set the pattern from which that Divine Intelligence will create. Our actions tell the Cosmic Law of cause and effect what good or ill is to be meted out to us, and Divine Intelligence creates our bodies and formulates the conditions of our lives accordingly. Unless we learn through God-communion how to guide our actions rightly, we shall have to continue to weep and pray for the alleviation of our suffering, which in fact is self-imposed.

Therefore, the business that supersedes all other business in life is to be busy with God first. No accomplishment is possible without the power of Creative Intelligence borrowed from Him. And no assurance of freedom from painful effects of wrong actions is possible without God-attunement, which enables us to make the Cosmic Law work for our happiness.

Beholding the throes of birth, the travails of life, and the pangs of death—all of which are imposed upon us by our karma, the effects of our past actions—we should concentrate on roasting the seeds of karma, because roasted seeds do not germinate. Those who destroy past karma in the fires of meditation-born wisdom do not have to reincarnate against their will.

So do not forget to keep your most important of all daily engagements—with God. Go into deep meditative silence and commune with Him on the altar of the dawn, and in the temple of night, which hides you from material distractions. Become one with the Divine Sculptor and make of your destiny whatever you want it to be.

XXXVII

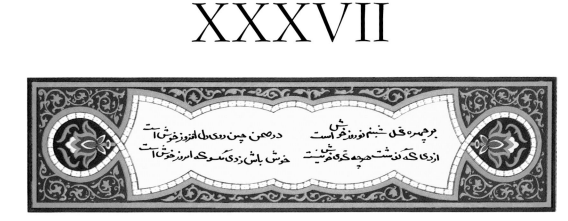

Ah, fill the Cup:—what boots it to repeat
How Time is slipping underneath our Feet:
Unborn TO-MORROW and dead YESTERDAY
Why fret about them if TO-DAY be sweet!

GLOSSARY—***Fill the cup:*** Intoxicate yourself with intuitive perceptions of God. ***What boots it to repeat:*** Of what use is vain regret? ***Time is slipping underneath our feet:*** The ceaseless and remorseless onward march of time. ***Unborn to-morrow and dead yesterday:*** In Cosmic Consciousness there is only the eternal present, without the illusion of past or future. ***To-day be sweet:*** The ever new bliss of God in the eternal now.

Spiritual Interpretation

Fill the cup of intuition with the divine wine of God-perception, and become intoxicated with His ever new bliss. Of what avail were the vain regrets that life is slipping away, all too soon to be lost forever? In Cosmic Consciousness you live in eternity, beyond the categories of time, without beginning or end, where past and future merge in the eternal now. In the realization of everlasting divine joy, yesterdays that once seemed so important exist not; nor are there unborn future tomorrows hiding in mystery. All cause for past remorse or future worry dissolves in the perpetual, sweet contact of the ever new divine bliss of Spirit, the Eternal Present, the only Reality.

Practical Application

Today fill the cup of life with all-round success. Forget the failures and trials of buried yesterdays, and frown not at the unborn fears of a future tomorrow. The regrets of yesteryears and anxieties about the future can be dispelled if all todays are lived correctly. After twenty-four hours, every today becomes a yesterday. Hence, by properly living every today, we can control the future and benefit by the past comprised of those todays.

Whether pursuing material success or spiritual upliftment, neither grieve over what you did not accomplish in the past, nor leave your efforts for success for tomorrow. Concentrate your best efforts to succeed today, and sooner or later they will be crowned with glory.

XXXVII

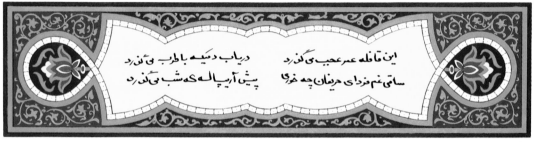

One Moment in Annihilation's Waste,
One Moment, of the Well of Life to taste —
The Stars are setting and the Caravan
Starts for the dawn of Nothing — Oh, make haste!

GLOSSARY — *One moment:* The first, negative state of ultimate divine realization. *Annihilation's waste:* An inner void, a negative state of absolute peace — Nirvana — which is the soul's first experience in deep meditation. *One moment:* The second, positive state of divine awakening. *The Well of Life to taste:* After feeling the negative void of inner peace, or Nirvana, to feel the deeper, positive state of union with Spirit as eternal ever new Bliss. *The stars are setting:* After the devotee reaches these divine states, his past karma, indicated by the position of the stars in his horoscope, begins to lose its control of his destiny. *Caravan:* The procession of the soul with its noble achievements and divine qualities. *Starts for the dawn of nothing:* From the beginning of the first or negative state of Nirvana, the soul then starts toward realization of Absolute Truth and attainment of freedom from rebirth.

Spiritual Interpretation

In the first moment of divine awakening, the soul is conscious of an inner void of absolute peace—the negative state of Nirvana, in which all worldly desires and mortal perceptions are felt as annihilated. Then another moment, by deeper contact with Spirit in ecstasy, the soul tastes the positive state of ever-new Bliss as it drinks from the Well that gives life to all creatures—the only well that can quench forever the thirst of all desires. In God-bliss, human karma is burned in the fire of the rising sun of wisdom; the stars lose their influence and no longer govern astrologically the destiny of that true devotee. The caravan of his soul qualities—intuition, love, self-control, ecstasy, inner joy, and all other divine attributes—assembles for the dawning of the highest state of God-union: liberation, in which cessation from compulsory re-birth in the misery-making world is attained. "Tarry not, true devotees, to indulge even in the joys of a rightly lived moral life; but speed your will and efforts to reach the Ultimate Goal, wherein the soul force is freed forever from mundane desires and resultant mortal bondage."

In the first state of divine awakening experienced by the meditating devotee, he finds he has become completely desireless and oblivious of all creation, but is yet not fully conscious of the ever joyous Spirit. This Nirvana, wherein all creation becomes dissolved in an inner void of perfect peace, is a negative but very high state of consciousness. It is the popular Buddhistic concept of Finality; but the Buddha did not mean that this was the ultimate state. The Hindu scriptures speak of a further goal, beyond that of a mere annihilation of desires. The final illumination of souls is a positive state of ever-existing, ever-conscious, ever-new Joy. True seekers should thus hasten on and on, from the simple joys of right living to the Nirvana state of desirelessness; and from that negative state to the positive spiritual state of union with the eternal bliss of the Absolute. In this state, the devotee finds that the seeds of his past karma have been roasted and destroyed by the sun of wisdom. He is freed forever from compulsory reincarnations. Any such liberated devotee can, of his own accord, come on earth to help man—as did Jesus and other great avatars—and at the same time maintain mastery over the cosmic forces that affect the lives of ordinary beings.

Practical Application

One moment life is beset with storm clouds of devastating troubles. Another moment the silver lining of success fringes the clouds of failures. Muster courage; keep peaceful within, calmly and righteously active without, and destiny will cease to gamble with your life. By continuous efforts at success, you will pass through the dark night of fate and troubles into the dawn of fulfillment, free from any clouds of calamity. Hasten to achieve this state of unshakable success.

XXXIX

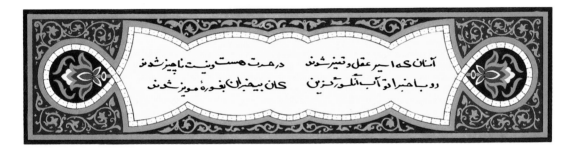

How long, how long, in Infinite Pursuit
Of This and That endeavour and dispute?
Better be merry with the fruitful Grape
Than sadder after none, or bitter, Fruit.

GLOSSARY—*How long:* Through the years of how many lives. *Infinite pursuit:* Engagement in the worldly activities of endless incarnations. ***This and that endeavour and dispute:*** Multifarious desires and the troublesome efforts and disputes to gain their objects. *Be merry:* Divinely joyful. *Fruitful grape:* The salvation-yielding bliss of God-realization. ***Sadder after none, or bitter, fruit:*** Have self-pity that no pursuit or interest in life occupies you, or that disappointment always results from the bitter aftertaste of sense pleasures.

Spiritual Interpretation

O devotee, why are you wasting time in endless pursuit of unquenchable worldly desires and accomplishments, struggling and disputing with others throughout incarnations for their attainment? Better to be divinely joyous and satisfied by intoxicating yourself with the salvation-yielding wine of ecstasy—God-realization. Otherwise, you may succumb to idleness from a sense of futility and have nothing; or you will continue to suffer from the bitter aftertaste of the fruits of earth-life desires.

Practical Application

It is foolish and unnecessary to pass life in sadness—the end result of disillusionment with the false promises of sense pleasures and material desires—when by contacting God in meditation you can fill the void of life with Divine Joy. When a sense of helplessness so grips the heart and mind that you feel like giving up all endeavors, or yielding to the way of the world though you know it will bring you unhappiness, seek that Divine Joy which gives meaning and purpose to life. Only in pursuit of that Joy can the endless yearnings of incarnations be fulfilled.

What is the use of struggling and worrying to gain what does not content you—pursuing those desires down endless avenues and blind alleys? Plan your life: Map out the path of your desires, that they lead to peace-yielding, mind-satisfying goals. It is useless to waste time in regretting lost opportunities, or in the inertia of indifference, or in trying to satisfy yourself with the taste of the bitter fruit of disappointing and only momentarily pleasing sense pleasures. Pursue the middle or balanced path in life, seeking the Creator as well as success and harmony with the plan of His creation. To commune daily with God in deep meditation, and to carry His love and guidance with you into all your dutiful activities, is the way that leads to permanent peace and happiness.

XL

من باده به جامی کئی خرام کرد   خود را به دو جام ی غنی خرام کرد

اول ـ طلاق عتی و دین خرام کرد   پس دختر رز را بزنی خرام کرد

You know, my Friends, how long since in my House
For a new Marriage I did make Carouse:
    Divorced old barren Reason from my Bed,
And took the Daughter of the Vine to Spouse.

GLOSSARY — *Friends:* Spiritual desires. *My house:* The body. *New marriage:* New realization of the forgotten eternal union of soul and Spirit. *Carouse:* Divine inner celebration, the joyous courting of Spirit in meditation. *Old barren reason:* Dry theological reason, which is based on sense experience, and is therefore barren, unable to produce God-realization. *Bed:* The couch of life on which rest all processes of consciousness. *Daughter of the vine:* Spirit-revealing, bliss-producing, intoxicating intuition.

Spiritual Interpretation

Omar introspects: "O my friendly spiritual desires, you know that for a long time in this bodily house my soul has been wooing the beloved Spirit, seeking a new, never-parting, all-surrendering union of body, mind, and inner being with the Divine. When I divorced from my couch of life the old favorite, theoretical reason, and espoused Spirit-revealing intuition, I realized that during bodily attachment I had only forgotten that I am already united to God, forever and forever."

Practical Application

The intellectual individual eventually becomes tired of his ever-disputing and discontented consort, reason. To find wisdom, he must divorce reason as the comforter of life and become espoused to the inner faculty of all-knowing intuition.

When reason dissatisfies you by failing to give you the promised offspring—the long-craved truth—then by daily meditation become betrothed to beloved intuition at the altar of silence within. Only then will you drink intoxicating bliss from your own intuition-born inner perceptions of truth.

XLI

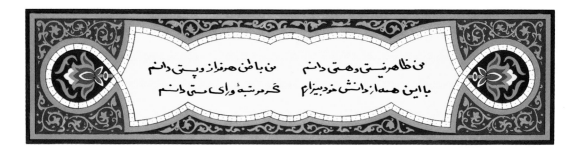

For "Is" and "Is-not" though with Rule and Line
And "Up-and-down" without, I could define,
I yet in all I only cared to know,
Was never deep in anything but—Wine.

GLOSSARY—**"Is":** The Being that is forever. **"Is not":** Matter, which appears real to the senses and yet is the changeable, illusory play of deluding forces and unreality. **Rule and line:** Theological dogmatism. **"Up":** The external—surface consciousness and matter. **"Down":** The internal—the realm of soul and Spirit hidden within human consciousness and matter. **Without:** Without "rule and line" or dogmatism; that is, by sheer logic. **Wine:** Intoxicating wine of divine realization.

---

* In Edward FitzGerald's revised second edition of *The Rubaiyat*, the reading of this quatrain is greatly clarified:
    For "Is" and "Is-not" though with Rule and Line
    And "Up-and-down" by Logic I define,
       Of all that one should care to fathom, I
    Was never deep in anything but—Wine.

Spiritual Interpretation

"By the rule and line of theological dogma and its fine distinctions, I could speak of God as 'Is' or Being, and of matter as 'Is not' or false appearance; and by sheer logic I could define and describe the surface ('up') states of human consciousness and the nature and laws of matter, and also the soul and Spirit hidden ('down') within them. Yet with all my theoretical, logical, and cosmological knowledge of scriptures, I know now that I never deeply cared for intellectual delving; I was never wholly immersed in anything but the wine of ecstasy."

Practical Application

No matter what beliefs or interests bind you, try to break those bonds and soar in the skies of inner ineffable freedom. There all mortal consciousness and the varied discords of the earth vanish, and you will be intoxicated by the endless, ever-satisfying wine of truth and new inspirations. Why take the surface details of life so seriously? Be drunk with the inner peace of divine realization, whatever your earthly lot.

XLII

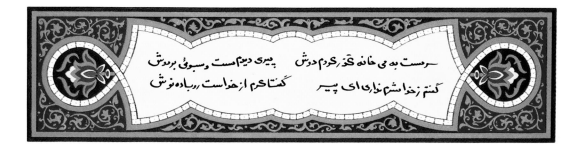

And lately, by the Tavern Door agape,
Came stealing through the Dusk an Angel Shape
Bearing a Vessel on his Shoulder; and
He bid me taste of it; and 'twas—the Grape!

GLOSSARY—*Lately:* After attaining Self-realization by meditation. *Tavern door:* The door of intuition in the caravanserai of superconsciousness. *Came stealing:* The subtle, very quiet way that spiritual perceptions come to the devotee. *Dusk:* Night of inner silence, the darkless dark background on which superconscious perceptions appear. *Angel shape:* Manifestation of God-consciousness. *Vessel:* The bottomless cup of wisdom. *Taste:* Permeate human consciousness with divine consciousness. *Grape:* Ever-new Bliss.

Spiritual Interpretation

After attaining Self-realization, as I sojourned in the caravanserai of superconsciousness—the first dwelling-place of the soul and its good qualities and higher inspirations on its march toward God—the Angel of God-consciousness came stealing through the open inner door of intuition in the darkless dark of my mental quietness. He bade me drink from his celestial vessel of beatific wisdom, filled with the grape of unending ever-new Bliss, and to permeate my life in the material world with its divine all-healing sweetness.

Practical Application

During your brief stay in the caravanserai of life, do not let worldliness and its endless worries possess you. Practice meditation and God-communion regularly, and you will taste the wine of joy and pleasantness all the time, no matter what your outer circumstances. Drinking the nectar of inner peace from the angel hands of your silent realization, you will drown the distractions and sorrows of your daily life.

XLIII

The Grape that can with Logic absolute
The Two-and-Seventy jarring Sects confute:
The subtle Alchemist that in a Trice
Life's leaden Metal into Gold transmute.

GLOSSARY—*The grape:* The bliss of God-contact and the Self-realization resulting from that communion. *Logic absolute:* Intuition, the omniscient faculty of the soul that fathers the reason of a man of Self-realization. *Jarring sects:* Contradictory theological teachings. *Subtle alchemist:* Divine consciousness, which subtly but surely and completely transforms worldly consciousness, as chemicals change the nature of metal. *In a trice:* Transcending the limitations of time, which governs the ordinary slow progress of man's evolution to higher consciousness. *Life's leaden metal:* Prosaic everyday life full of dark and heavy vexation. *Gold:* True and lasting happiness.

Spiritual Interpretation

The ever-new bliss and Self-realization born of God-contact bestow on the awakened soul the conviction of divine wisdom and intuition-saturated reason that can discern truth and settle all inner doubts arising from the contradictory theological teachings of various "isms." This divine consciousness, with its heavenly bliss, is the subtle alchemist that instantly transmutes the base lead of prosaic mundane life into the radiant gold of unending happiness.

Practical Application

In this quatrain, Khayyam again distinctly shows that the grape or wine has a symbolic meaning in his philosophy. No literal grape, nor the drinking of wine, could confute the contradictions of various theologies.

Self-realization alone can resolve all questions about truth, for it transcends the limited intellect and provides the proof of direct experience. It brings not only wisdom, but the joy of a peaceful attitude of mind. This even-mindedness, when maintained by regular deep meditation, removes the boredom, disappointment, and sorrow from everyday life, making it instead a very interesting and enjoyable experience of the soul.

XLIV

The mighty Mahmud, the victorious Lord,
That all the misbelieving and black Horde
  Of Fears and Sorrows that infest the Soul
Scatters and slays with his enchanted Sword.

GLOSSARY — *Mahmud:* Tenth-century warrior king. *Victorious lord:* The devotee who has conquered sense temptations and is lord and master of his own mind and its inclinations. *Misbelieving and black horde:* Ignorance, which produces darkness or error in the soul, causing doubt of the existence of God and of the superiority of good over evil ways. *Scatters and slays:* Wisdom first scatters the soldiers of darkness from the strongholds of the soul, and then destroys them. Through wisdom, all psychological weaknesses are driven out first, and ultimately the roots of all evils afflicting the soul are completely destroyed. *Enchanted sword:* Wisdom, from the all-conquering power of soul-revealing discrimination, which comes to the devotee through meditation.

Spiritual Interpretation

Like a victorious warrior, one who is lord of the self is a mighty conqueror of the senses. Using the divine ecstasy-enchanted sword of wisdom, that exalted devotee temporarily drives away and then ultimately destroys the doubt-creating soldiers of darkness: the fears, sorrows, and worries that invade the soul.

Practical Application

The kingdom of man's happiness is coveted by the celestial crusaders of wisdom and also by the soldiers of sordid sense lusts. Often the empire of inner contentment becomes the battleground of the opposing battalions of good and evil. The soul Prince of Peace should not remain inert, inactive in the face of this contest, but should train his army of discrimination in the art of combating the invading hordes of undesirable temptations. Thus supported by discrimination, the mentally strong man should drive away will-paralyzing fears and sorrows that invade the peace of his soul. He should remember that if Emperor Evil usurps his kingdom of contentment, its utter disruption will ensue. But if King Virtue is victorious, the peace in his kingdom of happiness will be unending.

This stanza of Khayyam's could have none other than a spiritual significance. The literal truth here stands before us, distinctly revealing Omar's underlying purpose in clothing his spiritual thoughts with the attractive garb of material imagery.

XLV

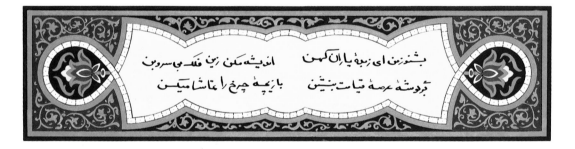

But leave the Wise to wrangle, and with me
The Quarrel of the Universe let be:
  And, in some corner of the Hubbub coucht,
Make Game of that which makes as much of Thee.

GLOSSARY—*Leave the wise to wrangle:* Let the intellectuals argue over conflicting theories. *Me:* The soul, with its all-knowing intuitive realization. *The quarrel of the universe:* The mysterious paradoxes of the universe, offering no answers to impatient queries. *In some corner of the hubbub coucht:* Sit in the nook of silence in meditation, deeply withdrawn from worldly distractions and mental restlessness. *Make game:* Don't take so seriously the mystery of life, which you cannot understand; enjoy it as a game or sport—the Lord's *lila*, as it is called in Hindu scriptures. ***That which makes as much of thee:*** The inexplicable laws of life that seem to sport so carelessly with our earthly existence.

Spiritual Interpretation

Let the theoretically wise argue the contradictions of theology. The secretive universe will go on mysteriously spawning its paradoxes without vouchsafing an answer to intellectual queries about its inexplicable conduct. The key to the cosmic conundrum is found not in the logical reasonings of the mind, but in the all-knowing intuition of the soul, the true Self.

Sitting in inner silence, deeply withdrawn from the distracting hubbub of the universe and restless mental gymnastics, meditate on the Infinite. But do not expect to understand all at once the universal riddle; the long-slumbering intuition of the soul awakens gradually at first. Meanwhile, do not take the tragedies of life so seriously. Look upon the cosmic drama as the Lord's *lila*, a huge sport in which life and destiny appear to enjoy gambling with you. In time, you will master the now inscrutable laws of the game and become the victor.

Practical Application

Do not join the crowd of intellectual theorists, each of whom espouses a different doctrine, conflicting with all others. No result will be gained, except doubt and confusion. To fathom the mysteries of life, enter the portals of silence and meditate deeply. Gradually you will reach the kingdom of Truth.

While you slowly and surely travel the path of realization, hold on to the inner peace of meditation throughout all activities. Do not get excited by taking life too seriously. Whether man be agitated or calm, life will pursue its own strange course forever. Worry, fear, discouragement, only add to the weight of daily burdens; cheerfulness, optimism, will power, bring about resolutions to problems. So the best way to live is to take life as a cosmic game, with its inevitable contrasts of defeat and victory. Enjoy the challenges as you would in a sport, no matter whether at the moment you are victorious or vanquished. Life goes on sporting with human beings irrespective of any conditions laid down by mortals. The truly wise are those who have understood with the soul's intuition, through Self-realization, the inexorable rules by which the cosmic game is played.

XLVI

For in and out, above, about, below,
'Tis nothing but a Magic Shadow-show
*   Play'd in a Box whose Candle is the Sun,*
Round which we Phantom Figures come and go.

GLOSSARY—***In and out, above, about, below:*** The perceptions of the three-dimensional sphere of creation. ***'Tis nothing:*** Matter is nothing but *maya*, cosmic delusion: the seemingly real forms are just as illusory as the images on a motion-picture screen, or in the mental motion-pictures of dreams. Dimensional perceptions in a dream are seen to be false on awakening; a person falling from a height in a dream finds, when he awakes, that he has not changed his position in space—he was the dreamer, not the dreamed. ***Magic shadow-show:*** The wonderful and artfully plotted motion-pictures of life. ***Played in a box:*** Exhibited on the stage of the universe—a "box" of finitude within the limitlessness of Infinity lying beyond this vibratory creation. ***Candle is the sun:*** As a little candle reveals the silhouette images of a shadow-show, as the sun lights the earth, so the spiritual "sun" of God's vibratory creative light causes the appearance of all images in our space-limited shadow-box of finite creation. ***Phantom figures:*** Echoing truths expounded by yogis of ancient times, science now confirms their realization that the physical forms of human beings are not the solid masses we perceive them to be, but electromagnetic waves—phantoms of light flitting about on the background of space.

Spiritual Interpretation

Just as motion-picture images of people, homes, mountains, stars, oceans, are unreal —electrical pictures of light and shadow projected on a screen—so human beings, moving about on this planet with its heavenly environment of sun and stars and island universes, are nothing more than passing phantoms of light seen on the screen of space, housed in the motion-picture hall of the cosmos. Life is as illusory as a magic shadow-show, whose candlelight within a box reveals silhouettes enacting entertaining dramas. The "sun" of subtle electromagnetic currents—the vibratory creative light of God—produces pictures of living beings, who suddenly appear on the stage of earth, and as suddenly mysteriously vanish.

This quatrain shows Omar's familiarity with the ancient Hindu concept of *maya* or cosmic illusion. *Maya* means "magical measurer": that which appears to divide the Indivisible into time, space, and form.

Practical Application

Life is transitory and unreal, like a picture show. Where are the vanished billions who lived during the last ten millennia? Where are the colossal kings and powerful men, such as Genghis Khan, William the Conqueror, Akbar, Napoleon? Where are our great-grandparents? Where will this mighty present population of the globe be a hundred years hence? Seek the One who is the Producer of this mysterious, constantly changing, ever-entertaining movie of tragedies and comedies. From His lips learn the meaning of the cosmic drama.

The sphere of creation with its manifestations within and without, above, about, below, can be duplicated by man in his dreams, which are mental movies, and are dissolved by wakefulness. Life is a macrocosmic mental movie-house of dreams, illusions of *maya*, which melt away in the wakeful state of ultimate wisdom. God-tuned sages have declared that the entire cosmos with all its complexities vanishes like a dream when the soul awakes in the eternal wakefulness of God. As a dream disappears when one is roused from sleep, so this cosmic dream dissolves when the devotee unites his consciousness with God's perpetual wakefulness.

Remember, then, that life is more than money, food, and raiment. Find friendship with your true Self, the soul, in the sanctum of daily meditation; and after deep communion with God in the bower of peace, give divine friendship and goodwill to all.

Let us not be idlers, labeling life an empty dream without having any real understanding of the truth. Since we have to eat, sleep, earn, and struggle, we should strive for the best in everything for ourselves and for all. Let us banish self-created nightmares of misery, brought on by selfish greed, sense slavery, and wars, and make a beautiful dream—if dream we must—of life's drama.

XLVII

خیام اگرباده پرستی خوش باش   باماه رخی اگرنشتی خوش باش

چون عاقبت کارجهان نامراهی شد   انگارکه نیستی چوهستی خوش باش

And if the Wine you drink, the Lip you press,
End in the Nothing all Things end in — Yes —
Then fancy while Thou art, Thou art but what
Thou shalt be — Nothing — Thou shalt not be less.

GLOSSARY — *Wine: Samadhi.* **Lip you press:** The merging of the individual soul with Spirit. **The Nothing all things end in:** Nirvana, Absolute Spirit; from which all things come and into which they merge again. **Thou art but what thou shalt be — nothing:** The true nature of man is not the mortal form but individualized, unmanifested blissful Spirit.

Spiritual Interpretation

Since the wine of *samadhi* meditation and the resulting union of soul and Spirit end in the consciousness of the Absolute state — Nothingness (No-thing-ness), or Nirvana, the vast spatial perception of the Infinite in which all things melt and hide — then realize that you have attained now, in this life, the complete Endlessness experienced by perfected souls. Even though material consciousness vanishes in *samadhi*, you are in tune with the ever-existing, ever-conscious, ever-new bliss of Absolute Spirit. That is the eternal Reality, of which you are an immortal part. Know, therefore, that you shall not, in all future time, be anything less than you are now. When the mortal form and realm of manifestation are transmuted into the "nothingness" or Nirvana of the Absolute, only illusions vanish; the unchanged Reality remains constant forever.

Practical Application

If, by glimpsing God, you have lost all zest for your material desires, but the inner bliss of Spirit is elusive still, do not feel forsaken and lonely in that temporary state of seeming emptiness. In time, the initial and deeper spiritual states experienced by the devotee will unite and end in the consciousness of Ever-New Joy. But in the beginning, there is a deep gorge between desirelessness and Ultimate Divine Joy. When you bridge that gulf by conscious communion with the Infinite Contentment, you will know you have reached that realm of realization which is free from all imperfection of disillusioning mortal pleasures that can never satisfy the soul. This Nirvana state is the complete extinction, by wisdom, of misery-making desires within the conscious and subconscious minds, thus destroying all chance of their enslaving recurrence. Then all your imaginings and expectations about the true nature of your being will be known and satisfied beyond your deepest dreams. You will find your oneness with Spirit more entrancing than anything pictured by your fancy throughout countless incarnations.

XLVIII

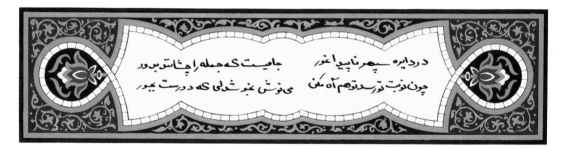

While the Rose blows along the River Brink,
With old Khayyam the Ruby Vintage drink:
*   And when the Angel with his darker Draught*
Draws up to Thee — take that, and do not shrink.

GLOSSARY—*Rose:* Divine bliss. ***River:*** The current of life force in the *sushumna*, the astral spine* insulated within the spinal cord. ***Old Khayyam:*** Ever-ancient Spirit; or

---

* The *sushumna* is the "spine," or channel of life, of the astral body, man's subtle body of light, *prana* or lifetrons; the second of three sheaths that successively encase the soul: the causal or ideational body, the astral body, and the physical body. The powers of the astral body enliven the physical body, much as electricity illumines a bulb. In *samadhi* meditation, when the consciousness turns within and flows into the *sushumna* stream of life, the yogi experiences a blissful superconscious state of spiritual awareness of the Divine Reality, the Cause and Substance of creation.

the consciousness of the guru, whose blessing and hoary wisdom guide the devotee into the realms of Spirit. *Ruby vintage:* Wine of *samadhi* (ecstasy). *Angel:* Christ Consciousness, which yoga treatises refer to as *Kutastha Chaitanya*, the infinite consciousness of God immanent in all creation. *Darker draught:* More deeply concentrated rapture, when the devotee transcends identification with the body and merges with the omnipresence of Spirit. *Do not shrink:* A bird long accustomed to a cage usually hesitates when presented with an opportunity to return to unfettered freedom. Similarly, a soul long caged in the body may waver when first offered the experience of joyous omnipresence in deep yoga meditation.

Spiritual Interpretation

As the yogi transfers his consciousness from the outer surface of the body, where tempting physical sensations are experienced, to the inner river of life flowing through the *sushumna* in the spinal canal—a river redolent with the sweet fragrance of the raptures of meditation—he drinks the wine of superconscious *samadhi* in communion with the ever-ancient Spirit. In this superconscious ecstasy, the yogi's consciousness is still in an individualized state: the devotee as a separate being experiencing the bliss of divine realization and God-communion. In deeper meditation, when the devotee's soul meets the angelic Christ Consciousness, with its ever-new intoxicating elixir of oneness with the omnipresence of God, he should not be fearful that he will lose the consciousness of himself in the freedom from consciousness of the body, the earth, and other material limitations. Rather, if he will drink of that deeper, expansive ecstasy of Christ-consciousness—courageously escaping the fleshly cage to unite with Omnipresence—he will find in this new state of *samadhi* his true Self, which resides universally in all things and manifests as his little self.

Practical Application

Follow the inspirations of wisdom given to you by Omar, secreted in his poetic teachings. If you sincerely do so, then the Inner Angel of your soul will offer for your unending enjoyment the deeper wisdom of personal God-contact to enlighten your being with Self-realization. If the wine of Omar's poesy intoxicates you, then be not apprehensive about drinking the transporting wine of yoga *samadhi*, about which he speaks, and which is brewed within the practicing yogi's exalted and purified being.

XLIX

ازروی حقیقتی نه ازروی مجاز مالعبت کنیم ونقد لعبت باز

بازیچه همی کنیم برنطع وجود رفتیم بصندوق عدم یکیک باز

'Tis all a Chequer-board of Nights and Days
Where Destiny with Men for Pieces plays:
Hither and thither moves, and mates, and slays,
And one by one back in the Closet lays.

GLOSSARY—*'Tis all:* This world with its drama of human lives. *Chequer-board of nights and days:* As a checkerboard consists of alternate white and dark squares on which chessmen representing rulers and their underlings are moved about, so does the rotating earth with its alternating days and nights form a grand checkerboard on which are played the lives of human chessmen. *Destiny:* The cosmic plan based on the law of cause and effect, which governs the activity and outcome of all things and all men. This scientific law is also called the law of karma; its operation explains those circumstances that are popularly misinterpreted as fortuitous happenings. Sudden agreeable or disagreeable events are generally accepted as acts of a blind fate, their causes not being known to most individuals because of lack of wisdom, or ignorance of the workings of the cosmic law. *With men for pieces:* Sentient beings under the influence of prenatal, reincarnated habits (karmic tendencies brought over from past lifetimes) are like chessmen moved by the hand of "fate" or unseen causes. *Hither and thither moves, and mates, and slays:* Men are moved from one state or condition to another throughout their lives, and are often thwarted in purpose, unable to carry out their plans. Finally, their existences are cut short by the transition called death. "Mate" (short for "checkmate") is a chess term signifying that one's king is in check and cannot move out of it; that player then loses the game. Fool's mate, scholar's mate, smothered mate, etc., all have the same end result, differing only in the moves made on the chessboard.

Therefore, the word "mate" in this quatrain means to be confounded, thwarted, frustrated, baffled, or defeated. ***Back in the closet lays:*** Just as each chess piece, after being played and captured, is put away, so human beings, after being gambled by destiny, are retired to an intermediate state, or astral heaven, between incarnations.

Spiritual Interpretation

The earth with its alternating days and nights of light and darkness is like a mysterious checkerboard on which the inscrutable law of cause and effect plays with human lives as chessmen. This mighty law of karma moves each person to lower and higher positions during his various incarnations; maneuvers him through victories and defeats, joys and sorrows; and withdraws him from the checkerboard of life when his time is up in the cosmic game. As chess pieces that have been "captured" are put back in a box as they are removed from the board, so karmic destiny, after gambling a life for a time, secretes that soul in the "closet," or resting place—the astral world, or heaven—until it is called forth in a new incarnation to face new challenges and to have a fresh opportunity to win the Ultimate Victory.

Practical Application

Man should look upon his life as though engaged in an interesting game of chess. A player, whether victorious or vanquished, should remember that he is playing just for sport. He ought not to allow himself to be thrown off balance by uncontrollable excitement when victorious nor by despondency at the advent of failure. The philosophical man of discrimination looks upon the tragedies and attainments of life with a serene mind, knowing his existence to be nothing more than an entertaining and educational game of concentrated skill.

Almost everyone likes a variety of comedy and tragedy in a novel, or in a play on the stage or screen; and as champion chess players enjoy a long, challenging game with both thrilling victories and staggering defeats, so should life be enjoyed, with all its contrasting circumstances. While undergoing the changes from youth to old age; during delightful experiences of meeting true friends, or the doleful trials of parting with them in death; when rejoicing in the company of loved ones, or suffering bereavement at losing them, the mind should be riveted to an inner ever-joyous attitude that this present life is not the finality, and that all things work for each human being's

ultimate highest good. The mysterious but just law of karma that removes beings one by one from the checkerboard of life also brings about a reunion of friends and loved ones during temporary retirement to the astral heaven and in succeeding new incarnations. True relationships are never lost forever in the oblivion of the phenomenon of death.

So when destiny maneuvers the game of your life through advances, stalemates, and retreats, it should be remembered that these effects are from causes you yourself have created in past lives. You should neither curse fate for your sorrows nor hail luck as the progenitor of your good fortune, but recognize your own hand in the turning of events in your life. If you are unhappy with your self-created destiny, remind yourself that God has given you the power of free choice to change that fate. Protracted efforts at right action produce gradual benefits; but if in addition you unite your will with God's wisdom through deep meditation, you will know instantly the real meaning of freedom.

L

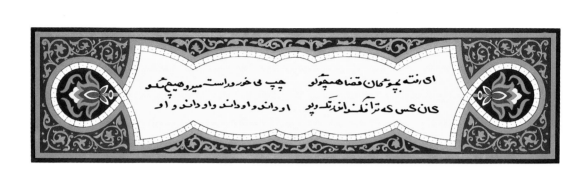

The Ball no Question makes of Ayes and Noes,
But Right or Left as strikes the Player goes;
And He that toss'd Thee down into the Field,
He knows about it all—HE knows—HE knows!

GLOSSARY—***The ball no question makes of ayes and noes:*** Human lives hurled and struck by karma have no freedom of will to guide their course, but must move helplessly in the direction in which they are sent. ***Right or left:*** The righteous path or its opposite, the evil path. ***As strikes the player:*** As ordained by the law of causation (karma) which creates good or bad tendencies in the present mental state according to habits acquired in the past of this life or previous lives. ***He that toss'd thee down into the field:*** God who created you and placed you on this planet. ***He knows about it all:*** God alone, with His eye of wisdom, perceives the way your life travels to the good or the bad path according to your past and present motives and actions. He alone knows what you will make of your life in the future. He alone knows truly all of your lives from beginning to end, from the first emergence of your ego, to its ultimate re-absorption in Him—the reunion of the soul with God.

Spiritual Interpretation

Like a ball whose course is set once it leaves the hand of the player, the ordinary man whose life is governed not by the free choice of true wisdom but solely by the cosmic law of causation—the hidden player of the game of life—loses his independence and cannot say *yes* or *no* when hurled by karmic compulsion to the evil path or the righteous way. God alone, who tossed man into the field of active earth existence, knows the entire course and direction of each human life as it moves along good paths or bad, according to the effects of past actions of this life and of previous incarnations. The Creator, being omniscient, omnipotent, and omnipresent, knows the beginning, middle, and end of all human lives.

Practical Application

The lives of most men, controlled not by self-determining wisdom but by strong habits and past-life tendencies,* are like balls tossed at the behest of the player, the law of cause and effect, or karma. As a ball has no choice, or free will, and must proceed in the direction in which it is sent, so already-formed habits—the sum total of man's second nature—drive their human victims into chalked-out and prescheduled lines of action.

Such men, governed by their habits, are like slaves and thus have no true freedom of choice. Once a habit is formed, it is bound to control its creator. Habits push souls willy-nilly into predetermined and predictable channels of behavior.

Very few persons understand that habits formed in past lives influence their present lives. Most are unaware of the silent and secret control of human destiny by past-life propensities hidden mysteriously in the subconscious mind. Hence they become fatalistic, not comprehending the reason when sudden good or bad crops up in their conscious mind, attracting good or bad experiences.

Those persons who find their lives out of their control, gambled with by hidden karma, should meditate and commune with God and know from Him, through the voice of intuition, the way out of that slavery. When puzzled by vagrant visitations of sudden misfortune or fortune they should by deep meditation seek the solution in the wisdom of God, wherein are written the answers to all the mysteries of human existence.

* Referred to in Yoga philosophy as *samskaras*, impressions of actions carried from one life to the next, manifesting their effects as strong tendencies or compulsions forming, as it were, man's present character or "second nature."

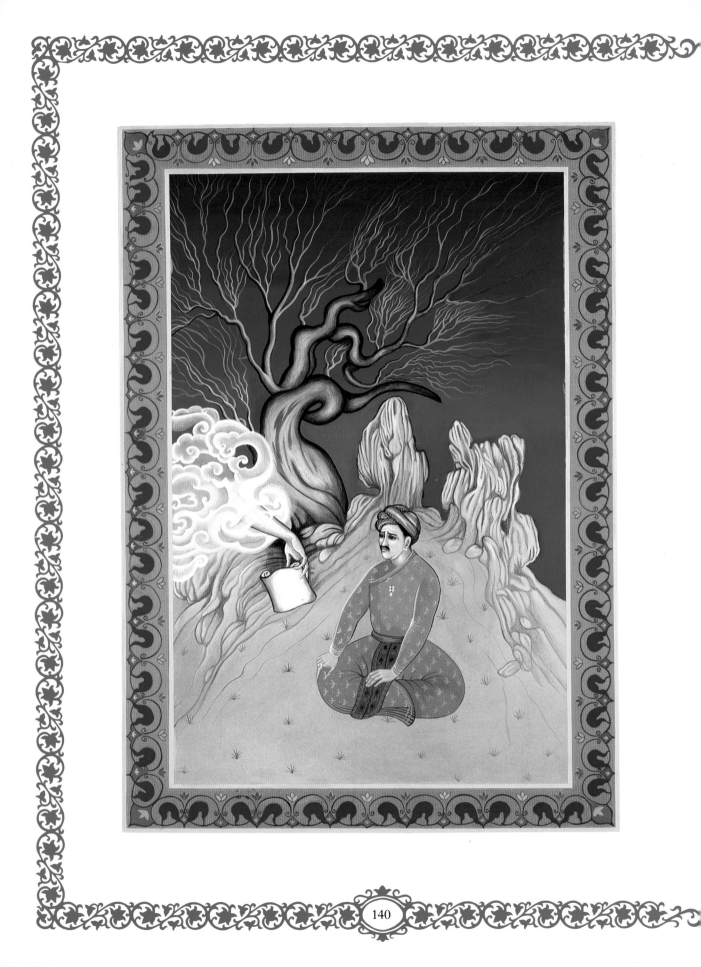

LI

برلوح تاں بودپنهان بودست   پیوسته قلم زنیه وبد آسودست

ازر تقدیر آنچه بایست بواد   غم خوردن وکوشیدن ناسودست

The Moving Finger writes; and, having writ,
Moves on: nor all thy Piety nor Wit
 Shall lure it back to cancel half a Line,
Nor all thy Tears wash out a Word of it.

GLOSSARY—*Moving finger writes:* Cosmic law, which is omnipresent and active in all creation, sets and guides the natural order of all things and creatures, and fixes man's destiny according to his individual karma (results from his own past actions). *Having writ, moves on:* Operates ceaselessly to set the course of the moments in man's life and the cycles of the universe. *Nor all thy piety nor wit lure it to cancel half a line:* Neither moral nor intellectual offerings can appease the cosmic law. *Nor all thy tears wash out a word:* Nor are a man's tears of fear or remorse sufficient to change the cosmic order; nor to eradicate the just karmic effects of past causes that he himself has set into motion.

Spiritual Interpretation

Cosmic law writes the destiny of all things in the cosmos. It ordains the natural order in the universe as applicable to each cycle in the spiral of evolution; it directs the cause-effect destiny of each man according to his actions in the present and previous incarnations. Having fixed the course of these changes in any one given time, the cosmic law moves on, moment to moment, cycle to cycle, to determine and issue subsequent decrees. Once cosmic law, in consonance with the Divine Will and with the karmic effects of man's actions, has thus determined the sequence and nature of events in the universe and in a man's life, no mere moral living nor any theological reasoning nor piteous tears can alter those mandates. Nothing can commute those consequences except God-realization, which alone transcends the laws of nature.

Practical Application

This quatrain does not emphasize the fatalistic viewpoint that unalterable decrees govern man's destiny. Rather, by inference, it warns unwary people that they should not remain satisfied that a little morality or scriptural knowledge or tears of rebellion will suffice to alter an undesirable destiny or justify the seeming vagaries of life. Attempts to remove unwanted conditions from one's life, and to remain unaffected by the conundrum of creation, will be effective only by acquiring Self-realization through God-contact.

Cosmic law is not a whimsical tyrant that works without rhyme, reason, or divine wisdom. Behind the delusive facade of universal order is the omniscient will of God. And operative in man's life, this Will as cosmic law ordains only those results that are already laid out by man according to his own past choice of right or wrong actions. He has to reap the results of those actions, until he changes himself spiritually and realizes the divinity of his inner Self. Only by realizing his unity with the One in whose image he is made does he become free, as is the Lord Himself, from cosmic imperatives and from bondage to the karmic effects of his own past actions.

LII

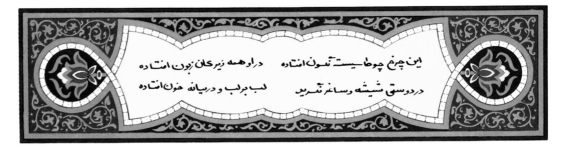

And that inverted Bowl we call The Sky,
Whereunder crawling coop't we live and die,
Lift not thy hands to It for help — for It
Rolls impotently on as Thou or I.

GLOSSARY — *Inverted bowl we call the sky:* The celestial canopy limited to a shape like all created things. ***Lift not thy hands to it for help:*** Do not wait for astrological influences to aid in changing your destiny. The symbolic planetary pattern of your birth was drawn by your own past actions. Call not on any outside or environmental power, but on the Maker of the heavens and earth, for deliverance and true freedom.

Spiritual Interpretation

"If you implore help from the blue heavens or guidance from the circling stars, you are foolish, for the heavens themselves are performing their exact movements in conformity with the decrees of cosmic law, the law by which your own karma (past actions) ordained the selfsame planets to shed their specific influences on you. Not the stars, but your own efforts to contact God, the Creator of the stars, will be effectual in changing your mortal destiny."

Practical Application

The stars are symbols of the governing or restraining influences of our own past karma. We should seek help only from Almighty God and our own will power, unceasingly striving to surmount our difficult material, mental, and spiritual problems.

Stars and human lives alike are governed by the cosmic law of cause and effect. Thus it is foolish for us to wait for destiny to change its mechanically operating, unalterable decrees. By adopting, in the present, the antidotes to our past, baneful actions, and by the unlimited help of God through meditation, we can nullify the dictates of our past deeds. What we have already done we can undo, or at least modify, by special acts of our will and by meditation, whereby our consciousness becomes suffused with a Higher Power.

Since stars symbolically influence our lives according to a certain pattern drawn by our consciously initiated past deeds, the best course we can pursue is to consciously adopt actions that will counteract the evil effects of our past misdeeds.

A great many people become foolishly fatalistic and resolve to do nothing until the planetary positions change. While it is not unwise to initiate good projects in astrologically auspicious hours, nevertheless it should be fully remembered that if anything is done with full faith in God it will be blessed with more auspicious influences than can ever be given by the favorable aspects of the stars.

LIII

With Earth's first Clay They did the Last Man's knead,
And then of the Last Harvest sow'd the Seed:
Yea, the first Morning of Creation wrote
What the Last Dawn of Reckoning shall read.

GLOSSARY—***Earth's first clay:*** The first embodied souls who, lured by earth's sensory temptations, became caught in karmic bonds of material desires and wrong actions. ***They:*** The effects of desires and actions. ***Last man's knead:*** From the first man to the last, the law of karma shapes each person's present incarnation, in a process of transmutation of primary principles through evolving cycles until the individualized soul reclaims its oneness with Spirit. ***Last harvest:*** The accumulated effects of one's life stored in the consciousness of man during the after-death state between incarnations. ***Sow'd the seed:*** The seed of karma and desires sown in the soil of a new incarnation. ***First morning of creation:*** Original precipitation of Spirit into matter. ***Last dawn of reckoning:*** The present incarnation of each man as he receives the effects, or judgment, of his past karma.

Spiritual Interpretation

Since the time of the first souls on earth who succumbed to the desire-producing temptations of the sensory world, the karmic effects of man's desires and actions have been the determining power in shaping each human's destiny, incarnation after incarnation. From the "last harvest"—each person's after-death state, comprising the stored, cumulative effects of all his desires and actions from his last life—the seed of unfulfilled karma and desire is gathered and sown in the soil of a new body in a new incarnation on earth. Verily, from the beginning of creation, the principle of karma was written as cosmic law in the book of life. It determines the exacting judgment read to each man in the "last dawn of reckoning"—the effects of his own free-will initiated past actions that confront him now in his present existence.

Practical Application

Life is the shadow of Spirit. Even as Spirit is eternal, so its shadow, the cosmos and the microcosm of man, perpetuate themselves in seemingly endless evolutionary cycles. All life is interlinked; the laws governing the cosmos also govern man. Like a seed, life yields a plant of human form containing within it another germ of life. The perpetual sequence of cause and effect, called the law of karma when applied to man, is the prime mover of the continuity of life expressed in earth's cycles and in man's recurrent reincarnations. There are many souls, or individualized sparks of Spirit, born in the earliest morning of creation, who began in lower forms of life and due to the slow process of evolving out of ignorance, are still roaming in the "last dawn" or manifestation of reincarnation as ordained in the book of cosmic karma.

Why be a helpless seed of life, continuously planted and replanted in the soil of time by cosmic law, undergoing all the hardships and storms of mundane existence? Use the Divine Intelligence within you to transcend karmic law. From the gleanings of life within you, harvest the precious seed of devotion, and sow that in the pristine garden of Spirit. There grow into a vine of love twining eternally about the divine Tree of Immortality.

LIV

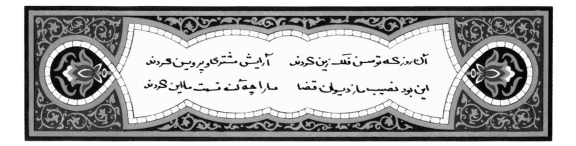

I tell Thee this—When, starting from the Goal,
Over the shoulders of the flaming Foal
Of Heav'n and Parwin and Mushtara they flung,
In my predestined Plot of Dust and Soul.

GLOSSARY—*Starting from the Goal:* Emanating from God, who is the Goal of evolutional creation as well as its Source. ***Over the shoulders of the flaming foal:*** Riding the stallion of fiery cosmic energy. (Pegasus, the Winged Horse, is a northern constellation in the sky, below the Pleiades and close to the vernal equinoctial point. Omar was an able astronomer.) ***Parwin and Mushtara:*** Persian terms for the Pleiades and Jupiter. The Pleiades contain Alcyone, the star that the ancients considered to be the central pivot of the universe. Jupiter is the planet of spiritual insight. ***Dust and soul:*** Man as the creature is dust, because subject to limitations of creation or nature, but as soul he is beyond all subjugation, one with the eternal freedom of the Creator.

Spiritual Interpretation

"In my cosmic vision I beheld my own and others' beings first emerge from the fiery source of Cosmic Energy. I perceived that God, according to His perfect plan, had preordained our individualized existence in a perishable body and an undecaying soul. He designed the body to have a definite human form and the soul to be stamped with His Imperial Image of Perfection. Having made us in His image, God gave us reason and freedom of choice to identify ourselves either with the sacred soul, temple of Spirit, or with the gross body of sense-temptations, which subjects man

to the circumscriptions of nature, its law of cause and effect (karma), and the influences of the environment and universe in which he resides. The Heavenly Father placed us on the stage of this cosmic delusive drama with the hope that we would use our power of free will to forsake the lesser joys of the flesh and return to Him in the finer perceptions of the soul."

Practical Application

The stars in the heavens with their silent influence, the orderly evolution of life, the cosmic laws of nature — all were arranged to accommodate the advent of man through whom the evolutionary cycle back to God would ultimately be culminated. Although the Heavenly Father predetermined man's perishable gross bodily form and his blissful soul, He did not preordain our individual human behavior either to cast Him away or to enthrone Him in our hearts.

Animals are like puppets, mostly activated by their instincts. They are predestined to live and behave in a certain limited way. The cow of the present day is practically the same in its mental development as its predecessors of twenty centuries ago. But man, though of fixed bodily limitations, has the ability to expand limitlessly the expression of his soul. The average modern man is more introspective and advanced than the average man of twenty centuries ago.

Hence, in spite of the limitations imposed upon us by nature, we should strive continually to expand, until we fully recover the consciousness of the forgotten perfect image of God within us. We must march on unceasingly until we regain that perfection and reach the Goal from which we started.

LV

چون مزد ازان بود مراآنکه کرد   بر من نخست درس عشق املاکرد
وانگاه تراضه ریزه قلب مرا   مفتاح خزاین درمعنی کرد

The Vine had struck a Fibre; which about
It clings my Being—let the Sufi flout;
Of my Base Metal may be filed a Key,
That shall unlock the Door he howls without.

GLOSSARY—**The vine:** The consciousness and life force that traverse the spine. The spine is like a tree, with roots above in the brain, and branches of efferent and afferent nerves below. The vine of consciousness in the ordinary man is planted in earthly desires in the brain and senses and should be transplanted to the soil of divine consciousness. **Struck a fiber:** Struck a new root in the soil of Cosmic Consciousness. **Clings my being:** The meditating yogi finds his consciousness clinging around the spinal region where the finer forces and God-consciousness reign. **Let the Sufi flout:** Omar did not use the word "Sufi" in this stanza, as Omar himself was a Sufi (a member of a devout religious sect including many great saints). FitzGerald, the translator of Omar, used the word "Sufi" here, erroneously identifying a Sufi as a materialist. FitzGerald omitted the word "Sufi" in all later editions. **Base metal:** The precious substance of life abused by material habits. **Filed a key:** The key of Self-realization fashioned by meditation. **Unlock the door:** Open the bars of the bodily prison into the kingdom of omnipresent freedom in God-perception. The limited body-perception is changed into limitless God-perception through meditation techniques. **He howls without:** The staid theologian, or a person who is only theoretically religious and does not live the true spiritual life, ridicules the possibility of personal God-realization; he remains "outside" in material consciousness with its doubts, fears, and discontentment, unable to enter the inner heaven of God-communion and direct perception of truth.

Spiritual Interpretation

"Like a vine, my consciousness and life force have ascended the spinal tree of seven divine centers and struck a new root deep in the soil of Cosmic Consciousness. My life and being cling round this vitalized spinal tree, nourished by its flow of spiritualized life force and consciousness. I know—not by theory, but by realization—that the vine of my consciousness has been transplanted from the soil of material desires into the soil of Cosmic Consciousness, wherein its roots have become fixed. I have proved that out of the debased, evilly used metal of my life, a key of Self-realization may be filed by meditation which, through the awakening of spinal consciousness, will unlock the door leading out of the bodily prison, from finitude into Infinitude and unlimited freedom. Most theoretically religious theologians who do not practice the true science of meditation deride the possibility of reaching the Infinite through the opening of the mystery door of the spine; outside of which, they must remain buffeting the discontentment and untold misery of the storm of materialism."

Practical Application

Theoretical religion is only superficially satisfying; its supports give way under the stress of tests. True religion is the actual experience of God. Man came from God, but lost Him midst the dazzling desires of the world; and this loss is the cause of all human grief and suffering. As man descended from transcendental Spirit into the body and the sensory world, when his life and consciousness flowed down and outward through the seven subtle cerebrospinal centers, the door to this inner kingdom leading back to God became locked by materialism.* It cannot be opened by theorization and blind belief. It is better to forge by scientific meditation the key of Self-realization, which alone will unlock the door to inner God-communion, rather than remain outside in material consciousness, unable to reach God with useless loud theological lamentations of dissatisfaction.

* As Christ taught: "Neither shall they say, Lo here! or, lo there! for, behold, the kingdom of God is within you" (Luke 17:21).

LVI

به ز آنکه بمحراب کنم بی نماز باتو بخرابات اگر کویم راز
خواهی تو مرا بسوز و خواهی بنواز ای اول و ای آخر خلقان همه تو

And this I know: whether the one True Light,
Kindle to Love, or Wrath consume me quite,
One glimpse of It within the Tavern caught
Better than in the Temple lost outright.

GLOSSARY — *This I know:* The certainty of unerring intuition. *The one True Light:* The Lord as Divine Wisdom, the one and only true wisdom in contrast to the world's many-sided false intellectualizations. *Kindle to love:* To quicken, through divine contact, universal compassion and the desire to serve all. *Or wrath consume me quite:* Or the divine contact might create in me discontent with everything mundane, and thereby engender a desire to forsake worldliness and all things material. Divine wisdom begets Self-realization by consuming the sense of "I" or the ego. *One glimpse of It:* One glimpse of the Divine in meditation. *Within the tavern:* In the caravanserai of earthly life and the mortal body, where soul, thoughts, and experiences gather for a little while. *In the temple lost outright:* To be lost in the theological and ceremonial trappings of religion, never dreaming of actually contacting God, the Dweller in His temples. Those who spend their lives merely discussing theology are "lost outright" from the path of God-realization.

Spiritual Interpretation

"I know this to be truth, that whether the contact of the one true light of Divine Wisdom infuse me with universal sympathy and humanitarian desire to serve all, or whether it fill me with righteous indignation toward worldly consciousness, inflaming me to consume my ego and material desires and renounce all things—I care not. But I am certain that it is far better to have even a flash of Cosmic Consciousness within the tavern of the mortal body, where the soul and thoughts temporarily sojourn, than to be lost in fascination with the outer temple of theology, behind which God hides—undiscoverable."

Practical Application

Just one glimpse of the Great Revelation is nectar to the soul, enlivening it to a divine quest for Self-realization—whether through expansion of the self in service to all, or through inward seeking on the path of renunciation of interest in all worldly matters. It is more gainful to contact the Infinite even once than to stray endlessly on the paths of theoretical discussion about God. Theologians are often pitifully near God in His temples, and yet so far from Him, if they have not actually found Him in the taverns of their daily lives. A single contact with God in meditation imparts to the devotee more wisdom, bliss, and contentment than many lives spent in theological theory and its inherent compromises and dissatisfaction.

LVII

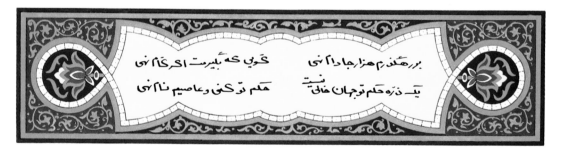

Oh, Thou, who didst with Pitfall and with Gin
Beset the Road I was to wander in,
Thou wilt not with Predestination round
Enmesh me, and impute my Fall to Sin?

GLOSSARY — *Thou:* The erroneously guided pseudo-soul or ego. *Pitfall:* Snare of ignorance and mental quagmires of wrong habits from which it is very difficult to extricate the soul. *Gin:* Sense-pleasures, intoxication with which stupefies the consciousness of the spiritual aspirant. ***Beset the road I was to wander in:*** Obstruct the path of wisdom and Self-realization. ***With predestination round enmesh me:*** With fallacies try to keep me stationary in and bound to my faults, making me think God has predestined me to be a prisoner of evil or of the law of karma. ***And impute my fall to sin:*** "Put the cart before the horse," i.e., reverse the established postulate of cause and effect. Since good or evil karmic tendencies cannot arise without having been first developed through man's free choice, each person is responsible for his own destiny.

Spiritual Interpretation

The Soul says: "O my error-stricken Ego, with the self-created snare of delusive ignorance and the intoxication of sense-pleasures you obstructed the road of wisdom on which I was to wander through earthly experiences to freedom. It is through your erroneous choice that my divine path is barricaded.

"I hope you will not lay the blame for my falling into the pit of ignorance to predestination or to God's law of karma (actions of the past of this or other lives) or to satanic delusion. You must not find excuses in order to evade the blame that belongs to you alone as originator and perpetrator of wrong actions."

Practical Application

Many people, because of inherent inclinations and the advantageous or disadvantageous circumstances into which they were born, wrongly think that God has arbitrarily predestined them to be either good or bad. But even though, in truth, one is virtuous or vicious owing to tendencies he himself acquired in the past of this life or in the past of many lives, the error-stricken one should not excuse himself by saying: "I am inclined to be bad because of the compulsions of instinct and my karma." This thought is dangerous, for few try to resist evil if they reason in this way. Evil habits are created only by one's own misuse of the free choice of will. Hence, wrong temptation, no matter how strong, can be counteracted by right discrimination and will power, and by courageous acknowledgment of accountability for one's faults.

No one should seek subterfuges and excuses for continuing in evil ways, blaming fate, Satan, or karma. Assuming full responsibility for all his shortcomings, one should endeavor to rid himself of them as expeditiously as possible.

LVIII

ای واقف اسرار ضمیر همه کس   در حالت عجز دستگیر همه کس
یا رب تو مرا توبه ده و عذر پذیر   ای توبه ده و عذر پذیر همه کس

Oh, Thou, who Man of baser Earth didst make,
And who with Eden didst devise the Snake;
For all the Sin wherewith the Face of Man
Is blacken'd, Man's Forgiveness give—and take!

GLOSSARY — ***Thou:*** Satan of Ignorance. ***Man:*** Beings, created in God's image. ***Of baser earth didst make:*** Converted the divine man into an inferior worldly being. ***Eden:*** The unalloyed state of original felicity. ***Didst devise the snake:*** Contrived the coiled force of creative energy that flows outward into the body from a subtle center at the base of the spine, rousing sex and the senses to substitute for the inflowing consciousness of divine ecstasy and communion with God. ***All the sin:*** Transgressions against social and divine laws arising from yielding to the temptations of Satan, and resulting in dire karmic consequences. ***Face of man is blacken'd:*** The mortal nature of man is desecrated and darkened with ignorance, obscuring the divine image of the soul within. ***Man's forgiveness give—and take:*** Man should not attribute all his misfortune to Cosmic Delusion, but blame also his own response to it. But Satanic Delusion must be admitted as a great factor in keeping man subject to sense temptations; therefore, the judgment of man according to karmic law should not be without recourse to some measure of compassion.

Spiritual Interpretation

"O Satan of Ignorance, by material temptations you have changed man, made in the image of God, into an inferior worldly being. O Evil Force, it is you who, in order to fight against the heavenly virtues of peace and self-control, devised

the alluring but happiness-poisoning, oft-misused creative force that lies coiled like a snake in a subtle center at the base of the spine, and which when flowing outward into the body, enticed by your temptations, rouses sex and the senses. Since you blackened with evil thoughts the divine image of man, you know he is not solely responsible for his faults; thus you should forgive his evil, committed at your instigation, by mitigating the judgment of your karmic law of retribution, and crave from man in return his forgiveness of you!"

Practical Application

Even though man has some responsibility for yielding to temptation and wrongdoing, it is Satan, symbol of Cosmic Delusion, who is the deviser of the snake of hypnotic sense temptations. It is he who has created greed, selfishness, sex temptations, anger, egotism, and hate, to counteract the divine creations of self-control, unselfishness, soul bliss, forgiveness, humbleness, and love. Hence, man is to be pitied that he is subject to so many inner and outer temptations against which he has but little warning of wisdom.

LIX

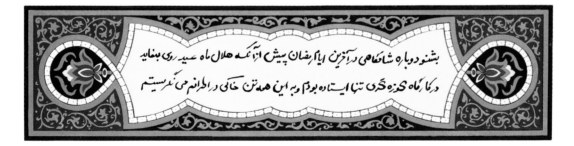

Listen again. One evening at the Close
Of Ramazan, ere the better Moon arose,
In that old Potter's Shop I stood alone
With the clay Population round in Rows.

GLOSSARY—*Ramazan:* An Islamic holy month of prayer and fasting for the purpose of contacting God; in this quatrain, symbolizing meditation. ***Ere the better moon arose:***

Before the spiritual inner eye opened. ***Potter's shop:*** God's creation. ***I stood alone:*** I remained in the outer loneliness of silence. ***Clay population:*** Mortals, subject to death and change, living but a short while on earth. ***Round in rows:*** The various karmic stages of man's development that determine his present placement in the world.

Spiritual Interpretation

"Hear ye, that one evening at the close of meditation, before the moon of inner insight arose in the firmament of my consciousness, I introspected in the loneliness of silence; and in the dim darkness of my mind, I glimpsed the presence of the Creator who has fashioned the numberless souls encased in the clay of transient flesh—each one placed in its respective environment according to its confining physical, mental, and spiritual karmic pattern."

Practical Application

After meditation, in the twilight of half-wisdom, one can continue to feel the presence of the Creator who has fashioned the temporal bodies of human beings, and thus strive to foreswear the passing allurements of the world and seek the Everlasting Life.

LX

And, strange to tell, among the Earthen Lot
Some could articulate, while others not:
And suddenly one more impatient cried—
"Who is the Potter, pray, and who the Pot?"

GLOSSARY—***Earthen lot:*** Countless individuals born on earth. ***Some could articulate:*** Some people can speak with wisdom. ***Others not:*** Others live in dark ignorance. ***One*** *more impatient:* One roused by introspection and spiritual hunger. ***The Potter:*** The Creator of human beings. ***The pot:*** The bodily vessel.

Spiritual Interpretation

It is a mystery to the ordinary mind why some people can translate human experience and nature in terms of wisdom, while others live in relative ignorance. Now and then from among the multitudes a man stirs himself from the stupor of ignorance by the exercise of discriminative introspection and a yearning for truth, and cries out the impatient question: "Who is the Creator of this body and what is the mystery of existence?"

Practical Application

This earth is a medley of the wise and the ignorant. Very few understand the paradox that some are born with the potential of keen intelligence and the power to articulate their thoughts, and others are dull-minded, lacking in understanding and the ability to properly express themselves. The wise know that all signs of intelligence or ignorance in human beings that are present from infancy are the result not of an arbitrary decision of God, but of specific tendencies cultivated by these individuals in former lives.

When God has given free will equally to all men, He cannot be accused of creating some with mental deficiency and others with brilliant minds. The different qualities of mentality and intelligence are created by man's exercise of his free will. Each individual then carries over his good or bad acquisitions from one life to another.

From the delusion-driven masses, a few rare souls become awakened through introspection and spiritual hunger to pray and meditate eagerly, exploring the nature of the Creator of the body and its mysterious mechanism and purpose.

LXI

باهیست که عقل آفرین می زنوش
صدبوسه زمهر برجبین می زنوش

این کوزه گر دهرمچین جام لطیف
میزد وباز برزمین می زنوش

Then said another—"Surely not in vain
My Substance from the common Earth was ta'en,
That He who subtly wrought me into Shape
Should stamp me back to common Earth again."

GLOSSARY—***Then said another:*** Another inquirer into Truth questions. ***My substance:*** The chemical and mineral elements of my body. ***From the common earth:*** From the earth, which is the common source of all physical bodies, and of their substance. ***He who subtly wrought me into shape:*** The Creator who with infinite wisdom formed, chemicalized, and animated the human body out of the cold clod, so that it glistened with life. ***Stamp me back to common earth again:*** Reconvert the body into the formless earthen clay from which all bodies are molded and into which all bodies will ultimately resolve again.

Spiritual Interpretation

"Surely God has a good reason why He magically transforms the products of the soil into living, feeling flesh and, having shaped the human form, reconsigns it to inorganic matter."

It is said that God is sleeping in the sod, dreaming different colors in the glistening gold, shining silver, rainbow gems, and motley minerals; and that He lies awakened in silent repose on the soft couch within the heart of blossoms as an aromatic fragrance, inviting all to seek Him, hidden beneath a quilt of petals. He is roused to active life and audible voice in the instinctive alertness of animals and the sweet songs from the throat-flutes of the thrush and nightingale. He gives His first intelligent utterance in the laughter and wails of the human baby and the independent reason-guided actions of the adult. At last His omnipresence and omniscience find full expression in delusion-free Christs and supermen.

Thus, pure Spirit, after creating from Itself an illusion of matter, shrouds Itself behind matter. Inherent in the origin of matter from Spirit is the attraction of matter to reform itself into Spirit again. The grossest manifestation of matter, in which Spirit first expresses Its presence, is the inert life of minerals—base metals and precious stones. Plants are the next finer form of matter, in which life begins to stir as Spirit manifests Its tenderness in the flowers. In the succeeding higher forms of matter, Spirit moves and experiences in sentient animals; and thinks, reasons, and creates in man, with his unique brain and numberless attributes of mind. In avatars like Christ, the Spirit, encased in a body, is able to resolve the matter of that body into omnipresent Spirit again, as demonstrated in Christ's resurrection.

The Spirit in the ordinary man is unable in one lifetime to sufficiently refine the flesh into Spirit, therefore that particular bodily clay is returned to the dust of its earthly origin, and a new body is formed for the continuing progression of Spirit— incarnation after incarnation. That is the way of spiritual evolution. But in supermen the Spirit is able to expand Its individual soul-self, and transform the body as well, into the magnificent Eternal Substance. It was to demonstrate the Spirit-nature of all matter that Jesus was resurrected in body as well as in soul, and why Spirit as Jesus can alternately rematerialize that body at will at any time and anywhere, and dissolve it again in Spirit.

Practical Application

Throughout a cycle of manifested creation, Immortal Spirit undertakes a long journey of evolution through inert matter to animate, sentient, and intelligent life forms. Of all the wonders in the Lord's creation, the greatest marvel is how He converted through this evolution the unfeeling clod into sensitive flesh able to manifest the soul, the individualized Spirit within. To the nonunderstanding observer, it is strange that when the soul has finished its allotted experiences in the body, the body is again returned to its original state of inert matter. But to the enlightened one, who sees all forms as manifestations of Spirit, the body is just a temporary convenience for the use of the soul during its mortal sojourn. When the soul has finished its dinner of experiences on the paper plate of the body, that no longer useful implement is cast away and replaced by a fresh one. Why view this as tragedy? Life is mysteriously interesting.

LXII

اجزای پیاله که درهم پیوست   بشکستن آن روانی دارد دست

چنین سرودست نازنین ازسرت   ازهر که پیوست وبین که شکست

Another said – "Why, ne'er a peevish Boy,
Would break the Bowl from which he drank in Joy;
Shall He that made the Vessel in pure Love
And Fancy, in an after Rage destroy!"

GLOSSARY — ***Another said:*** Another person reasons. ***He that made the vessel:*** God who created the body, the vessel of life. ***In pure love and fancy:*** With His great divine love and tender imagination. ***In an after rage destroy:*** Suffering and death are not attributable to the loving Father of all, to whom we mistakenly ascribe the passions of man.

Spiritual Interpretation

Another truth-seeker reflects within himself: "Why, it is unnatural for even a petulant child to willfully break the cup from which he derived joy in quenching his thirst. So I doubt that He who is the God of Love acts in irresponsible anger to destroy the bodily vessel of life that He Himself created through His delicate divine imagination, and from which He drinks the love and devotional offerings of tender human hearts. God, being all-wise, must have good reason for the advent of death as well as the creation of life."

Practical Application

Death comes for one of two reasons: (1) when the nectar of ultimate divine wisdom has been fully quaffed from the Holy Grail of life, or (2) when the law of karma (cause and effect) so ordains. Death by disease or accident is the fruition of stored seeds of evil actions in the past; it is not caused arbitrarily by God. Only an ignorant mind would accuse God of wrathful vengeance when a man brings untimely death upon himself by his own evil karma.

God is the Cosmic Fountainhead of limitless Love. It is foolish for man to think of Him as even less sensitive than a perverse child who has the sense to regard kindly the vessel from which he has happily quenched his thirst. When man beholds the *danse macabre* around him, he should not attribute its cause to God. As a free agent, man brings either salvation or suffering upon himself according to his own past actions. The effects of those actions are stored in the archives of his subconsciousness as either good or bad proclivities and habit tendencies, just waiting for the right conditions to express themselves. Whenever misfortunes visit man, therefore, he should blame only himself for having invited them by his own past actions and self-created tendencies.

LXIII

None answer'd this; but after Silence spake
A Vessel of a more ungainly Make:
"They sneer at me for leaning all awry;
What! did the Hand then of the Potter shake?"

GLOSSARY—*A vessel of more ungainly make:* An ill-favored or wicked individual. ***For leaning all awry:*** For my mental and physical deformities. ***What:*** How is it my fault that I have such defects? ***Did the hand then of the Potter shake?*** Is it not by some mistake that my Creator made me thus?

Spiritual Interpretation

"No ignorant person can understand, even after much silent reflection, why he suffers deformity in body or mind. 'Ah, people are offended by my deficiency, and I must endure my state along with scorn and pity. But I do not see how the blame is mine. Somehow, perhaps, the Creator blundered when he was shaping me.' "

The wise man, on the other hand, realizes by introspective communion that his physical or mental deficiencies cannot be attributed to a just and loving God. Even citing heredity as the cause of all good or bad human tendencies does not support the justice of God. Why should some souls attract a good heredity and be born with healthy bodies, noble tendencies, and efficient brains, while others attract a bad heredity and are born with physical handicaps, evil tendencies, and wrongly inclined brains? The truth is, a man inherits good or evil in one life inasmuch as he had stored good or evil karma from his actions of former lives.

Practical Application

Physical, mental, or spiritual imperfections sprout from hidden prenatal seeds of one's own past evil actions or offenses against the exacting laws of God and Nature. Those who are ignorant of the just law of cause and effect are often moved with self-pity, and blame their Creator for the evils that afflict them. A sufferer of shortcomings should blame neither God nor fate, but should reconcile his mind to the truth that one attracts misfortune through his own forgotten misdeeds in the past.

This does not mean that one must therefore resign himself to his karmic state; nor should he harbor feelings of guilt for being the cause of it. Each new lifetime—each moment of that lifetime—is a God-given opportunity to reconstruct one's life ideally. Limitation and defeat must never be accepted. The ever perfect soul within will express itself more and more through every opening made possible by the right use of will and discriminative free choice. The truly admirable are those who transmute adversity into a personal victory.

LXIV

Said one—"Folks of a surly Tapster tell,
And daub his Visage with the Smoke of Hell;
They talk of some strict Testing of us—Pish!
He's a Good Fellow, and 'twill all be well."

GLOSSARY—*Folks of a surly Tapster:* Human beings who conceive of their Creator as an imperious tester of men—a dispenser of harsh judgments, drawing bitter drafts from the casks of human lives. *Daub his visage with the smoke of hell:* Picture the Creator as a God of vengeance and wrath. *They talk of some strict testing of us:* Ignorant people maintain that it is the Creator who causes His children to suffer by inflicting cruel tests. *'Twill all be well:* As the beauties of creation bespeak the goodness of the Creator, let us develop faith, by experience in God-realization, that all created things move on toward a divine goal of bliss.

Spiritual Interpretation

"There are people who depict their Creator as one who imperiously tests man with the smoke of ignorance and the fire of punishment, and who judges man's actions with heartless scrutiny. They thus distort the true concept of God as a loving, compassionate Heavenly Father into a false image of one who is a strict, unsparing, and vengeful tyrant. But devotees who commune with God know it is foolish to think of Him otherwise than as the Compassionate Being who is the infinite receptacle of all love and goodness. As God, the Father of the Universe, is good, all things must end well with His children; they and all creation are moving to a glorious climax and reunion in Him."

Practical Application

Learn from the loving care with which God has fashioned every living creature that He is no angry despot, but a Father of tenderest compassion who treasures each member of His house of earthly life. Anomalies are not the work of God, but are karmic results of man's inharmony with divine law. The punishments that result from evil are not intended as persecutions, but to serve as stimuli to remind us to avoid evil and seek good. The wise know that tests are meant to "make us, not break us." God's laws of creation beset us with difficulties to bring out from within us our divine potential. By the Lord's omniscient design, we have been endowed with human intelligence capable of pushing aside all obstacles and marching ahead to the plenary goal of goodness.

The wise therefore say to have contempt for your trials; for even though your intelligence and free choice are inexorably subject to stringent testing, the truly striving soul will find victory and happiness in the end because God is good and His good purpose is lurking behind the countless perplexities of life.

Draw on God for the solution of all your problems. Do not allow your courage and quick wit to be paralyzed when overwhelming difficulties suddenly come down on you like an avalanche. Keep awake your intuitive common sense and your faith in God and try to find even the slenderest means of escape, and you will find that means. All will come out right in the end, for God has hidden His goodness behind the superficiality of the paradoxes of mortal experiences.

LXV

Then said another with a long-drawn Sigh,
"My Clay with long oblivion is gone dry:
But, fill me with the old familiar Juice,
Methinks I might recover by-and-by!"

GLOSSARY — *A long-drawn sigh:* An expression of an effort of courage roused to conquer a difficult problem. *My clay:* My hoary immortal soul identified throughout its many past incarnations with a mortal physical form and its material perceptions and desires. *With long oblivion is gone dry:* With long forgetfulness of the soul's divine nature as it passed through the glooms and joys of past lives. *Fill me with the old familiar juice:* Infuse me with the primordial intuitive wisdom so familiar to the soul, and hidden deeply within it. *Methinks I might recover:* I may thus regain my lost remembrance of my true soul consciousness of perfection and bliss. *By-and-by:* Gradually, through steady spiritual endeavor.

Spiritual Interpretation

Then another sane seeker, with a mixed sigh of hopelessness permeated with courage, deliberated within himself: "The expression of my soul, having for aeons of incarnations been identified with its contact of flesh and a consequent dependence on the instrumentality of a physical brain for perceptions and experiences, has become dulled, forgetful of its spiritually ethereal nature—immortal, perfect, blissful. The 'soft-clay' resiliency of the intuition of soul perceptions has, over this period of time, become dried out and hardened into gross sensory impressions and desires; but could again be revived with the draft of soul wisdom poured from the cask of meditation. Let me thereby fill my arid consciousness with the soul's age-old intuitive God-perception, revivifying my matter-parched, long-forgotten divine soul nature. Surely, by deep and patient meditation, the flesh consciousness of matter and material desires will gradually be reformed into the lost soul perceptions of infinite, unending bliss."

Practical Application

How obdurate is mortal human consciousness! Its habit patterns of material pursuits and dependencies are stubbornly resistant to spiritual remolding. The spiritual aspirant hopeful of obtaining ultimate illumination must "take a deep breath" and summon courage for a long-drawn struggle to conquer flesh consciousness.

This principle is equally applicable to transforming any hardened karmic pattern. There must be unceasing determination in order to reshape incarnational bad habits and tendencies. Most people lose the pliancy of their will once they feel constricted by failure or ill-health habits. They can remodel their lives gradually by strong efforts to succeed and by drawing from the brimful soul-keg of ever-fresh inspirations within.

No matter how hardened the molded clay of the mind is, dried and scorched with failed efforts, it can be softened and reformed by renewed infusion of vitalizing courage and right effort.

LXVI

ماه رمضان برفت وشوال آمد هنگام نشاط عیش وقرآن آس
آمد که آنه خیمها اندرورش گوینذه پشت پشت حمال آس

So while the Vessels one by one were speaking,
One spied the little Crescent all were seeking:
And then they jogg'd each other, "Brother, Brother!
Hark to the Porter's Shoulder-knot a-creaking!"

GLOSSARY—*The vessels:* Reflective human beings; the bodily receptacles of all-wise souls. *Were speaking:* Introspecting. *One spied the little crescent:* One perceived in deep interiorization the omniscient spiritual eye of astral light. *All were seeking:* All who desire the realization of truth are seeking, consciously or unconsciously, the spiritual eye of wisdom with its all-knowing intuitive perception. *Hark:* Listen with deep attention. *The Porter's shoulder-knot:* God, the Divine Conveyer who shoulders all human vessels, which He has strung and interknotted with vibratory universal life. *A-creaking:* The sound of the Cosmic Vibration, God's creative power and cosmic life responsible for universal creation and the support of human lives.

Spiritual Interpretation

As these soulful truth-seekers expressed their wisdom thoughts, one, deeply penetrating, perceived the all-seeing astral eye of wisdom hidden in the forehead, the instrument of omniscience sought consciously or unconsciously by all who desire to behold truth. When kindred souls, stirred by one thus enlightened, similarly practice the divine science of interiorization, all proclaim to one another their common universal experience: "Behold through the eye of wisdom that God has bound all souls together with strings of pulsating, all-pervading Cosmic Life, which is resonant with the sound of the creative Cosmic Vibration."

Practical Application

All life is activity, and where there is activity there is vibratory sound. Hence, when God's power becomes creatively active, the vibration of His cosmic motor of creation emanates a cosmic sound, the great *Aum* or Amen. The wise, by calmness and meditation, can hear this creative vibration, alive with God's power and intelligence, rumbling behind all other sounds.

The second property of vibration is light. The all-pervading light of God from which creation emerges can be seen in man as the microcosmic spiritual eye, emanating the life and intelligence that creates and supports his individualized existence. No matter how many theological arguments man may hear or propound, truth is known when it is beheld through the hidden spiritual eye of wisdom. Those who attain this realization universally testify to the omnipresence of God as the Upholder of all universes and beings, strung together in infinite space by His vibratory power and cosmic life.

LXVII

چون فوت شوم بـاده شـوئيد مرا   تلقين ز شراب نـاب گوئيد مرا
هراهيوكه بروز حشر بينيد مرا   از خـاك در مـيكده جوئيد مرا

Ah, with the Grape my fading Life provide,
And wash my Body whence the Life has died,
And in a Windingsheet of Vine-leaf wrapt,
So bury me by some sweet Garden-side.

GLOSSARY—*The grape:* Cosmic perception. *My fading life provide:* Renew me with the youth, the ever-newness, of Spirit. *Wash my body whence the life has died:* With divine wisdom bathe my ego consciousness, in which material desires have perished.

In a windingsheet of vine-leaf wrapt: Protected by the power of divine perception. ***Bury me:*** Keep my physical ego under the control of Spirit. ***By some sweet garden-side:*** In the joy of cosmic consciousness, in which universal brotherhood—oneness with all life—is sweetly experienced.

Spiritual Interpretation

"As the egoistic, youthfully exuberant pleasures fade from my consciousness, O Heavenly Father, provide me with the grape of cosmic perception, renewing my life in Thy consciousness. Lave with purifying divine wisdom my once body-identified ego, from which material desires and attachments have all passed away. At the last, wrap my physical ego with the vine-leaves of divine experiences and let it rest hereafter in the garden of cosmic consciousness where only blossoms of noble qualities unfold."

When with the bestowal of wisdom the ego loses its limiting identification with the mortal and sensory consciousness of the physical body, its preoccupation with material desires and pleasures also fades away from one's life. Having shed its gross consciousness, enwrapping it in divine experiences and burying it in the garden of transcendent meditation, the renewed consciousness that remains is the invisible, or subtle, metaphysical ego. This spiritualized inner ego, or divine individuality, now becomes the ruling consciousness in one's life. No longer is one circumscribed by the selfish "I" and "mine." Rather, he brings forth from his meditations into his everyday life his cosmic perceptions of the omnipresence of Spirit. All his actions are virtuous and noble; his consciousness becomes universal, in a joyous unity with all life.

Ultimately, by the transforming power of cosmic consciousness, the spiritualized ego also fades away, leaving the pure soul which blends into the vastness of the Infinite Spirit.

Practical Application

Wisdom, acquired through discriminative living and deep meditation, will bring back the wasted youthfulness of the mind, grown tired and devitalized by life's trials.

Let our waning life be surrounded and strengthened by vital and noble experiences, and our mental and physical frailties be buried in the garden of sweet living friendship and loving service.

LXVIII

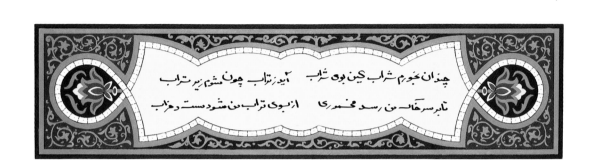

That ev'n my buried Ashes such a Snare
Of Perfume shall fling up into the Air,
As not a True Believer passing by
But shall be overtaken unaware.

[A continuation of the concept in the previous verse]

GLOSSARY—*My buried ashes:* My spiritualized or divine ego—the remnant or purified essence of my Spirit-consumed physical ego—resting in the garden of cosmic consciousness. *A snare of perfume shall fling up:* Will exude such an arresting spiritual aroma. *Into the air:* In my environment. *A true believer:* A seeker after God. *Passing by:* Even casually coming in contact with me. *Shall be overtaken unaware:* Will be subtly captivated and drawn toward God by the divine fragrance of my Spirit-expanded universal consciousness.

Spiritual Interpretation

"My transcendent spiritualized ego—the 'ashes' or purified essence of my physical ego that has been consumed by the fire of Spirit and buried in the garden of cosmic consciousness—will nourish the flowering of divine qualities and wisdom in my being, the subtle fragrance of which will in turn attract other seekers of Truth and draw them irresistibly to God."

When the little body-identified ego is spiritually transformed by divine perceptions and God-realization, that spiritualized consciousness becomes expansive and all-pervasive, like a wafting mystical fragrance that draws and inspires other seeking souls.

Such a transfigured being is a living garden silently beckoning to all and imparting to those who enter into its beauty a wondrously uplifting peace and joy.

The very fire of Spirit that transmutes in *samadhi* meditation the gross physical ego into its divine soul essence remains with that transformed personage as a radiating, alluring halo of light—a light invisible, yet unmistakably perceptible—attracting others into wisdom's everlasting luminosity.

Practical Application

Exchange in your life the repulsive noxious weeds of evil qualities for the charming, attractive flowering plants of noble qualities whose beauty and fragrance will inspire others to forsake their slovenly mechanical life and cultivate their own lovely living gardens. Transmute your weaknesses into vital spiritual strength that you may walk surely on the garden path of life that leads to God, helping others along the way whom you find wandering by the wayside in despondency.

LXIX

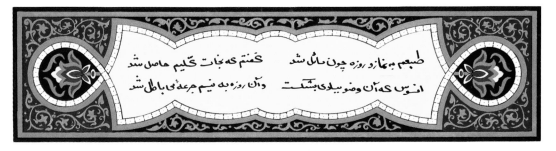

Indeed the Idols I have loved so long
Have done my Credit in Men's Eye much wrong:
Have drown'd my Honour in a shallow Cup,
And sold my Reputation for a Song.

GLOSSARY—*Idols:* Name, fame, sense pleasures—objects of the ego's veneration. ***Have done my credit in men's eye much wrong:*** Have obscured to myself and others my real soul-nature with its unlimited powers and supernal bliss. ***Have drown'd my honour***

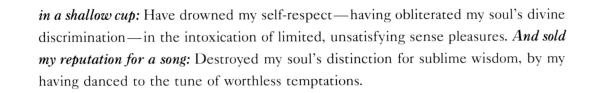

in a shallow cup: Have drowned my self-respect—having obliterated my soul's divine discrimination—in the intoxication of limited, unsatisfying sense pleasures. *And sold my reputation for a song:* Destroyed my soul's distinction for sublime wisdom, by my having danced to the tune of worthless temptations.

Spiritual Interpretation

"As is the wont of human nature, I have deified the desire for name, fame, and sense pleasures—'idols' worshipped by the ego—thereby losing the esteem of wise men and of my own convicting conscience. I have obliterated my soul's honor of divine discrimination by quaffing from the shallow cup of sense pleasures its intoxicating, unsatisfying draft. What perversity that I have foolishly bartered my soul's reputation of being all-seeing and ever-wise, for the temporary allure of the senses."

Practical Application

It is the foolishness of human beings that blunts the ignorance-destroying keen wisdom of the soul by idolatrous reveling in short-lived sense pleasures. Succumbing to the intoxicating wine and wild music of temptations, man subverts the soul's protective, honorable discrimination. Right judgment is the guiding light of the soul; never lose it by indulgence in injudicious pleasures.

LXX

Indeed, indeed, Repentance oft before
I swore — but was I sober when I swore?
    And then and then came Spring, and Rose-in-hand
My thread-bare Penitence apieces tore.

GLOSSARY—***Repentance oft before I swore:*** Regrets for my enslavement to the senses; swearing to renounce all inner weaknesses. ***But was I sober when I swore?*** But now I think I was only momentarily intoxicated with the short-lived inebriant of repentance and remorse. ***And then and then came spring:*** Fresh temptations ever arose. ***Rose-in-hand:*** Offering roseate hopes of new pleasures. ***My thread-bare penitence apieces tore:*** My oft-repeated, timeworn sorrow for my sins was rent once more.

Spiritual Interpretation

"The contention between repentance and indulgence is truly a psychological riddle. I always felt remorseful about my slavery to the senses just before taking a solemn oath to overcome my inner weaknesses forever. But when my sense-satiety abated, my repentance waned with it. I wondered if my avowal had been reasonable — was it made in a normal mental state or under the inebriating emotional influence of post-indulgence regrets?

"I stood between the two seasons of repentance-born resolutions and desire-instigated forgetfulness. After a hard winter of self-discipline, a springtime of new temptations gradually appeared, alluring me with fresh optimistic hopes of rosy physical pleasures. My garment of repentance, worn thin by self-denial, was tattered by these enticements and flung aside; and I surrendered myself to the seductive vernal call of the senses."

Practical Application

Wrong habits inevitably inflict physical and mental pain on their victims, prodding them to resist the influence of such evils. With sincere repentance of one's follies, there comes a determination to forsake them. But time wears off this resolution, as the repercussions of bad habits are forgotten. The mind becomes neutral and careless. At this juncture, the advent of temptations produces an overwhelming effect on the vulnerable individual, and he succumbs to the new lures of sensory gratification.

Whosoever would have a permanent safeguard against misery-making temptations must constantly strengthen his right resolves with positive thoughts and good activities; for abstinence alone only creates a negative consciousness of deprivation. There should be no relaxation of vigilance through a false sense of security or through mental rationalization. Watchfulness and introspection hold the serious penitent in readiness to banish temptation whenever it threatens the mental sanctuary of self-control.

LXXI

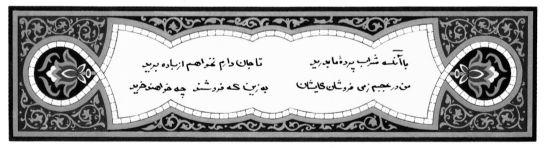

And much as Wine has play'd the Infidel,
And robb'd me of my Robe of Honour — well,
I often wonder what the Vintners buy
One half so precious as the Goods they sell.

GLOSSARY— *Wine:* Divine intoxication. *Play'd the infidel:* Caused me to relinquish my loyalty to sense indulgences. *Robb'd me of my robe of honour:* Deprived me of the praise of former, pleasure-mad friends with whom I had caroused. *Vintners:* Those who with the wine press of meditation produce some draft of spiritual realization. *The goods they sell:* The God-perception they lose in exchange for acquiring sense enjoyments.

Spiritual Interpretation

"By drinking the wine of divine inspiration, I have become a disbeliever in the joy of sense pleasures. Being thus spiritually disposed, and having renounced my former indulgences, I have lost, with no regret, the accolade of my sense-addicted, pleasure-mad erstwhile friends. I wonder at the foolishness of other devotees who work to produce the wine of spiritual perceptions and then sell those vintage joys for paltry coins of sense indulgence to buy spurious delights. Those folly-crazed ones, clutching their counterfeit treasures of sense, cannot obtain with them any of the precious divine joys they have sold for the sake of possessing short-lived sense enjoyments."

Practical Application

Devout persons who seriously and earnestly pursue the spiritual path may become objects of ridicule to the material minded, and thus lose soulless social prestige. Jesus spoke of this worldly condemnation of the righteous: "There is no man that hath left house, or brethren, or sisters, or father, or mother, or wife, or children, or lands, for my sake, and the gospel's, but he shall receive an hundredfold now in this time...*with persecutions;* and in the world to come eternal life."*

Sincere devotees who drink deeply of the intoxicating divine perceptions of God-communion see how foolish some spiritual seekers are who, being tempted by sensory lures or shamed by social critics, give up their Godly quest and again revert to the world-honored state of delusion. Those who thus sell their divine joy to acquire the imitation bliss of physical pleasures cannot obtain with the "coins" of that indulgence anything comparable to the true and everlasting Joy of God-realization they have relinquished.

* Mark 10:29–30.

LXXII

Alas, that Spring should vanish with the Rose!
That Youth's sweet-scented Manuscript should close!
The Nightingale that in the Branches sang,
Ah, whence, and whither flown again, who knows!

GLOSSARY—***That spring should vanish:*** The banishment of youthful earthly desires. ***With the rose:*** Along with fragrant flowery temptations. ***Youth's sweet-scented manuscript:*** The youthful follies and sweet dreams and ambitions recorded on the living pages of the brain. ***Should close:*** Is renounced. ***The nightingale:*** Wisdom. ***In the branches sang:*** Reverberated within all avenues of the mind. ***Whence:*** From eternal Spirit. ***Whither:*** Into eternal Spirit. ***Flown again:*** Expanded into omnipresent perception. ***Who knows:*** Known only by one who *knows.*

Spiritual Interpretation

From the earthly standpoint, it is viewed as sad when the young devotee gives up his freshly flowering material desires and shuns all fragrant sensory temptations. It seems pathetic to see him relinquish the roseate dreams and ambitions so charmingly written on the living pages of his young brain. But in so doing, the devotee finds the Cosmic Nightingale of wisdom emerging from eternity into the temple garden of his consciousness, warbling throughout the avenues of his mind its song of divine realization. The cosmic wisdom at first fills his individual soul, and then his wisdom-perception spreads into Omnipresence. He alone knows, because he *knows.*

Practical Application

Misunderstanding people hold in dismay those ardent souls who renounce material desires, sensory temptations, and even intellectual ambitions in order to give themselves completely to the search for God and truth. Yet adventurous persons are not afraid to expend their last coin to get back a larger treasure. No one finds success who is not willing to lose in order to gain, or who will not invest his savings to make a profit. Similarly, one should not shortsightedly refuse to relinquish small worldly advantages and delights for greater ones in Spirit. The assurance of this fulfillment is the testimony of those who have attained divine realization. Thus do the sages sing: "He who knows, he knows; none else knows."

LXXIII

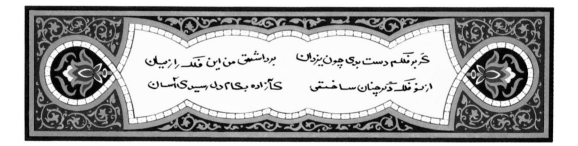

Ah, Love! could thou and I with Fate conspire
To grasp this sorry Scheme of Things entire,
Would not we shatter it to bits — and then
Re-mould it nearer to the Heart's Desire!

GLOSSARY—*Love:* God's Infinite Intelligence reflected in creation as Cosmic Love, the divine power of attraction and harmony. *Fate:* Cosmic Law, the universal principle of karma, cause and effect. *Sorry scheme of things entire:* The sad schedule of the intermixing of dualities throughout the cosmos — evil with good, death with life, sorrow with laughter. *Shatter it to bits:* Destroy all undesirable happenings on the earth. *Re-mould it nearer to the heart's desire:* Remake the scheme of life in this world according to the divine pattern of perfection secreted in the core of every soul.

Spiritual Interpretation

If man could but harness his innate divine will to God's pure Infinite Intelligence immanent in creation as Divine Love and to the Cosmic Law that governs all happenings through cause and effect, he could wield that wisdom and power to shatter the sad circumstances of karmically set patterns and remold the effects of earth's untoward dualities into circumstances nearer to the ideal plan that God intended. Thus does every being at times wish he could play the role of Creator and make this world more to his heart's desire. This longing for unalloyed happiness springs from the core of the soul in which is secreted the divinely inherent perfection and everlasting bliss of one's true being.

Practical Application

The world is a divine enigma—evil mixed with good, sorrow with joy, death with life. A sensitive person, helplessly suffering from the seeming vagaries of nature, often thinks wistfully of reshaping circumstances on earth according to his inner sense of justice and God-given conscience.

With love and law, which govern all life, man should attempt to change sorry happenings, and try with all his might to make the world a brighter, warmer spot in accordance with the heart's desire for a consummate existence. One who takes up this challenge may fail to accomplish quickly or fully the goals he sets; but that fact should not deter him from doing, even in a small measure, all he can to make the earth a better lodging place. Man is made in God's image; the potentialities of the powers of God are hidden within him. He should bring these dynamic attributes to the surface of his consciousness and use them to solve the purposely-made-difficult conundrum of life.

No one should blame God for the intrusion of adversities. The Lord's Divine Love and Law exist for the upliftment of all beings; it is man's transgressions that create inharmonies. The compassionate Creator has given man sufficient capability to conquer all his trials. If that were not so, He would not have made the tests and temptations of life so difficult. He designed this earth a seemingly sorry and knotty problem so that striving for its resolution would bring out of His children their latent indomitable power. When confronted with the troubles and obstacles that plague existence, the recourse is to arouse this unlimited invincibility sleeping in the mind. Working together, the children of God will be able to transform the conditions on earth into a joyous state.

Each individual, each nation, each world civilization is playing 365 dramas in a year. These various plays are what make the mundane theater very interesting.

If this world were already perfect and inhabited only by angelic beings, there would be no drama; its very existence would be unjustifiable. As everything is perfect in God, a perfect world apart from Him would be unnecessary. God's purpose was to create His human children in His image and endow them with intelligence and free choice by which they could cast Him away or accept Him. His hope is that His progeny will transcend their nature-born imperfections, discard earthly temptations, and use their free choice to find Him. His potentially perfect but outwardly deficient children have thus been put on this struggle-beset earth to learn to salvage from beneath the debris of superficial limitations their inherent divinity.

We should not rack our brains nor become disbelievers in a divine scheme in creation if we cannot understand all the paradoxical dramas of good and evil, of happiness and sorrow, of rich and poor, of health and sickness, of intelligence and stupidity, of peace and wars, of kindness and cruelty in nature. A successful play has suspense, captivates the interest, bewilders or puzzles, and ends with a satisfying dramatic flourish. Likewise, the extremely complex drama of the cosmos unfolds around God's impeccable motive, its purpose to be revealed to us sometime, somewhere.

If the aim of this panoramic play were grasped from the beginning, it would not speak well of the skill of the Cosmic Dramatist. How deftly He has hidden His spectacular finale behind the many gaudy screens of earth civilizations and individual lives therein. In the last act, in the after-death state, the perfected man beholds the Divine Playwright and then understands all that has gone before. Similarly, God will in time suddenly lift the veil for every ascending soul, disclosing the final part of the Cosmic Drama, long concealed behind the many acts of tragedies and comedies, to reveal its mighty, noble end.

LXXIV

Ah, Moon of my Delight, who know'st no wane,
The Moon of Heav'n is rising once again:
How oft hereafter rising shall she look
Through this same Garden after me—in vain!

GLOSSARY—***Moon of my delight who know'st no wane:*** The bliss of security in God, known only to the soul rescued from a transient cosmos. ***Moon of heav'n is rising once again:*** Phenomena of the outward universe, in contrast, are bound to alternations. ***How oft hereafter rising:*** Fettered, like all natural manifestations, to periodical recurrence. ***This same garden:*** The earth, planet of stately lilies, riotous weeds. ***Shall she look ... after me—in vain:*** Why seek an absolute omission? I am one with Spirit, subtle beyond material influences.

Spiritual Interpretation

"A changeless joy, born of lonely meditative search, is now my own, sound against the ages. The little earthly dollhouse, lit by playful Luna, cannot longer accommodate my being, spacious with omnipresence. Outmoded moon, seek me no further; I am gone with empyreal lightnings!"

Practical Application

Man should struggle to realize himself, not as a body confined to a point in space, but as the vast soul, which the ego, in most barbaric modes, conspires in vain to cramp.

[In his Autobiography of a Yogi *(Chapter 33), Paramahansa Yogananda comments further on this quatrain of the* Rubaiyat *in describing the state of the spiritually liberated soul:]*

The *Upanishads* have minutely classified every stage of spiritual advancement. A *siddha* ("perfected being") has progressed from the state of a *jivanmukta* ("freed while living") to that of a *paramukta* ("supremely free" — full power over death); the latter has completely escaped from the mayic thralldom and its reincarnational round....*

The "Moon of my Delight who know'st no wane" is God, eternal Polaris, anachronous never. The "Moon of Heav'n rising once again" is the outward cosmos, fettered to the law of periodic recurrence. Through Self-realization the Persian seer had forever freed himself from compulsory returns to earth: the "garden" of Nature or *Maya*. "How oft hereafter rising shall she look after me — in vain!" What frustration of search by a wondering universe for an absolute omission!

LXXV

And when Thyself with shining Foot shall pass
Among the Guests Star-scatter'd on the Grass,
And in thy joyous Errand reach the Spot
Where I made one — turn down an empty Glass!

GLOSSARY—***Thyself with shining foot shall pass:*** The expanded Self—all earthliness transformed into light—will realize omnipresence. ***Among the guests star-scatter'd on the grass:*** Astral vision sees souls shining within different bodies, strewn over the confines of this verdant sphere of earth. ***Joyous errand:*** The loving service rendered to humanity by a liberated soul. ***The spot where I made one:*** Cosmic Consciousness, where-

* Reincarnation is the doctrine that human beings, compelled by the law of evolution, incarnate repeatedly in progressively higher lives—retarded by wrong actions and desires, and advanced by spiritual endeavors —until Self-realization and God-union are attained. (See quatrain III.)

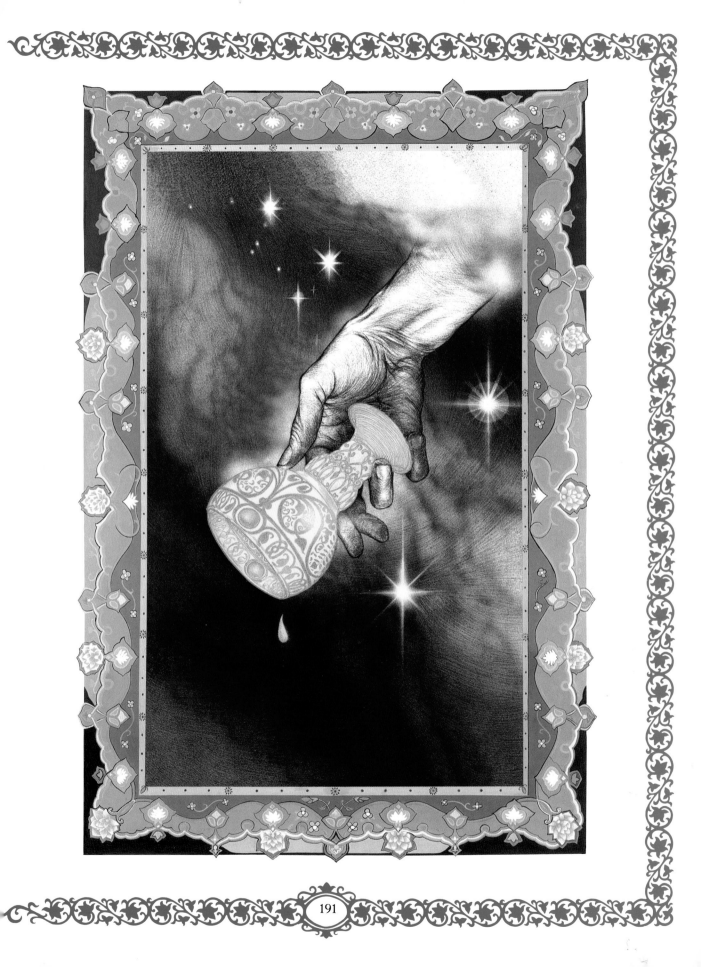

in the "I," the limited ego, becomes one with Omnipresence. ***Turn down an empty glass:*** The universe has been emptied of an ego whenever one more human being finds final refuge in Spirit.

Spiritual Interpretation

"O devotee, a time will come when your Self will lose all its earthliness and become eternal light, ever-burning radium, emanating infinite joy and understanding. Your soul, sailing through the luminous astral region behind the physical world with its millions of temporary guests, will bless all earth-dwellers among whom it passes, silently stirring and awakening them through the whispers of conscience. As your soul's little joy is transmuted into the limitless bliss of Spirit, it reverberates a liberating chant through all responsive, truth-seeking hearts. Your untrammeled spirit ultimately reaches the boundlessness of omnipresence, the core of Cosmic Consciousness, wherein the little body-confined ego vanishes, having become expanded into the Eternal Oneness. With the cork of ignorance thus removed, your freed soul, the image of God within you, will emerge from the heretofore confining bottles of its physical and astral bodies, to commingle forever with the cosmic sea of Spirit, in which it has long dwelt as a delusion-beset separate entity.

"Then shall the wine glass of delusive existence—emptied of its soul essence and never again to be filled through the coercion of *maya*—be now and forever turned down."

Practical Application

It does not matter whether or not one fully comprehends the day-to-day enigmas of life. What is important is to be resolute in the search for the True Happiness, the Joy that is the origin of one's being. The mortal becomes the Immortal by developing his full potential—physically, mentally, and spiritually. He attains illumination who follows steadfastly the cue of conscience and the counsel of sages, and who shares with other benighted souls his gathering wealth of wisdom and smiles. He is an inspiration and a bestower of upliftment for others who seek to behold the Hidden Light within themselves.

O mortal being, harken to the call of wise Omar Khayyam. It is thy divine destiny to strive unceasingly until the exalted inner state is reached wherein the little self

transcends all mental circumscriptions of body-consciousness, creed, and race, and merges as the greater Self into universal brotherhood with all life; and thence attains everlasting union with the One Life.

Thus is the ultimate purpose of life climactically described in this concluding *Rubaiyat* quatrain.

Addenda

Omar's Dream-Wine of Love

By Paramahansa Yogananda

Written by Paramahansa Yogananda in the 1930s, during the time when he was working on his interpretation of the Rubaiyat, *which later appeared serially in Self-Realization Fellowship's magazine. Sri Daya Mata, president of Self-Realization Fellowship and one of Paramahansaji's close disciples since 1931, was present at that time. She recalls that Paramahansaji was in a deep state of* samadhi *when these words flowed from his soul. He speaks first of his own spiritual search (and that of every devotee who has sought and found the Divine, including the God-intoxicated Omar Khayyam), and then from his at-one-ment with God as Love. Paramahansaji titled the piece "Omar's Dream-Wine of Love," with the subtitle, "A Scripture of Love."*

I sought love in many lives. I shed bitter tears of separation and repentance to know what love is. I sacrificed everything, all attachment and delusion, to learn at last that I am in love with Love—with God—alone. Then I drank love through all true hearts. I saw that He is the One Cosmic Lover, the One Fragrance that permeates all the variegated blossoms of love in the garden of life.

Many souls wonder wistfully, helplessly, why love flees from one heart to another; awakened souls realize that the heart is not fickle in loving different ones, but is loving the one God-Love that is present in all hearts.

The Lord ever silently whispers to you:

I am Love. But to experience the giving and the gift of love, I divided Myself into three: love, lover, and beloved. My love is beautiful, pure, eternally joyous; and I taste it in many ways, through many forms.

As father I drink reverential love from the spring of my child's heart. As mother I drink the nectar of unconditional love from the soul-cup of the tiny baby. As child I imbibe the protecting love of the father's righteous reason. As infant I drink causeless love from the holy grail of maternal attraction. As master I drink sympathetic love from the flask of the servant's thoughtfulness. As servant I sip respectful love from the goblet of the master's appreciation. As guru-preceptor I enjoy purest love from the chalice of the disciple's all-surrendering devotion. As friend I drink from the self-bubbling fountains of spontaneous love. As a divine friend, I quaff crystal waters of cosmic love from the reservoir of God-adoring hearts.

I am in love with Love alone, but I allow myself to be deluded when as father or mother I think and feel only for the child; when as lover I care only for the beloved; when as servant I live only for the master. But because I love Love alone, I ultimately break this delusion of My myriad human Selves. It is for this reason that I transfer the father into the astral land when he forgets that it is My love, not his, that protects the child. I lift the babe from the mother's breast, that she might learn it is My love she adored in him. I spirit away the beloved from the lover who imagines it is she whom he loves, rather than My love responding in her.

So My love is playing hide-and-seek in all human hearts, that each might learn to discover and worship, not the temporal human receptacles of My love, but My love itself, dancing from one heart to another.

Human beings importune one another, "Love me alone," and so I make cold their lips and seal them forever, that they utter this untruth no more. Because they are all My children, I want them to learn to speak the ultimate truth: "Love the One Love in all of us." To tell another, "I love you," is false until you realize the truth: "God as the love in me is in love with His love in you."

The moon laughs at millions of well-meaning lovers who have unknowingly lied to their beloved ones: "I love you forever." Their skulls are strewn over the windswept sands of eternity. They can no longer use their breath to say, "I love you." They can neither remember nor redeem their promise to love each other forever.

Without speaking a word, I have loved you always. I alone can truly say, "I love you"; for I loved you before you were born; My love gives you life and sustains you even at this moment; and I alone can love you after the gates of death imprison you where none, not even your greatest human lover, can reach you.

I am the love that dances human puppets on strings of emotions and instincts, to play the drama of love on the stage of life. My love is beautiful and endlessly enjoyable when you love it alone; but the lifeline of your peace and joy is cut when instead you become entangled in human emotion and attachment. Realize, My children, it is My love for which you yearn!

Those who love Me as only one person, or who imperfectly love Me in one person, do not know what Love is. Only they can know Love who love Me wisely, faultlessly, completely, all-surrenderingly — who love Me perfectly and equally *in* all, and who love Me perfectly and equally *as* all.

The Rubaiyat of Omar Khayyam

I

Awake! for Morning in the Bowl of Night
Has flung the Stone that puts the Stars to Flight:
*   And Lo! the Hunter of the East has caught*
The Sultan's Turret in a Noose of Light.

II

Dreaming when Dawn's Left Hand was in the Sky
I heard a Voice within the Tavern cry,
*   "Awake, my Little ones, and fill the Cup*
Before Life's Liquor in its Cup be dry."

III

And, as the Cock crew, those who stood before
The Tavern shouted — "Open then the Door!
*   You know how little while we have to stay,*
And, once departed, may return no more."

IV

Now the New Year reviving old Desires,
The thoughtful Soul to Solitude retires,
*   Where the White Hand of Moses on the Bough*
Puts out, and Jesus from the Ground suspires.

V

Iram indeed is gone with all its Rose,
And Jamshyd's Sev'n-ring'd Cup where no one knows;
*   But still the Vine her ancient Ruby yields,*
And still a Garden by the Water blows.

VI

And David's Lips are lock't; but in divine
High piping Pehlevi, with "Wine! Wine! Wine!
    Red Wine!" — the Nightingale cries to the Rose
That yellow Cheek of hers to incarnadine.

VII

Come, fill the Cup, and in the Fire of Spring
The Winter Garment of Repentance fling:
    The Bird of Time has but a little way
To fly — and Lo! the Bird is on the Wing.

VIII

And look — a thousand Blossoms with the Day
Woke — and a thousand scatter'd into Clay:
    And this first Summer Month that brings the Rose
Shall take Jamshyd and Kaikobad away.

IX

But come with old Khayyam, and leave the Lot
Of Kaikobad and Kaikhosru forgot:
    Let Rustum lay about him as he will,
Or Hatim Tai cry Supper — heed them not.

X

With me along some Strip of Herbage strown
That just divides the desert from the sown,
    Where name of Slave and Sultan scarce is known,
And pity Sultan Mahmud on his Throne.

XI

Here with a Loaf of Bread beneath the Bough,
A Flask of Wine, a Book of Verse — and Thou
    Beside me singing in the Wilderness —
And Wilderness is Paradise enow.

XII

"How sweet is mortal Sovranty!" — think some:
Others — "How blest the Paradise to come!"
    Ah, take the Cash in hand and waive the Rest;
Oh, the brave Music of a distant Drum!

XIII

Look to the Rose that Blows about us — "Lo,
Laughing," she says, "into the World I blow:
    At once the silken Tassel of my Purse
Tear, and its Treasure on the Garden throw."

XIV

The Worldly Hope men set their Hearts upon
Turns Ashes — or it prospers; and anon,
    Like Snow upon the Desert's dusty Face
Lighting a little Hour or two — is gone.

XV

And those who husbanded the Golden Grain,
And those who flung it to the Winds like Rain,
    Alike to no such aureate Earth are turn'd
As, buried once, Men want dug up again.

XVI

Think, in this batter'd Caravanserai
Whose Doorways are alternate Night and Day,
*   How Sultan after Sultan with his Pomp*
Abode his Hour or two, and went his way.

XVII

They say the Lion and the Lizard keep
The Courts where Jamshyd gloried and drank deep;
*   And Bahram, that great Hunter — the Wild Ass*
Stamps o'er his Head, and he lies fast asleep.

XVIII

I sometimes think that never blows so red
The Rose as where some buried Caesar bled;
*   That every Hyacinth the Garden wears*
Dropt in its Lap from some once lovely Head.

XIX

And this delightful Herb whose tender Green
Fledges the River's Lip on which we lean —
*   Ah, lean upon it lightly! for who knows*
From what once lovely Lip it springs unseen!

XX

Ah, my Beloved, fill the Cup that clears
TO-DAY of past Regrets and future Fears —
*   To-morrow? — Why, To-morrow I may be*
Myself with Yesterday's Sev'n Thousand Years.

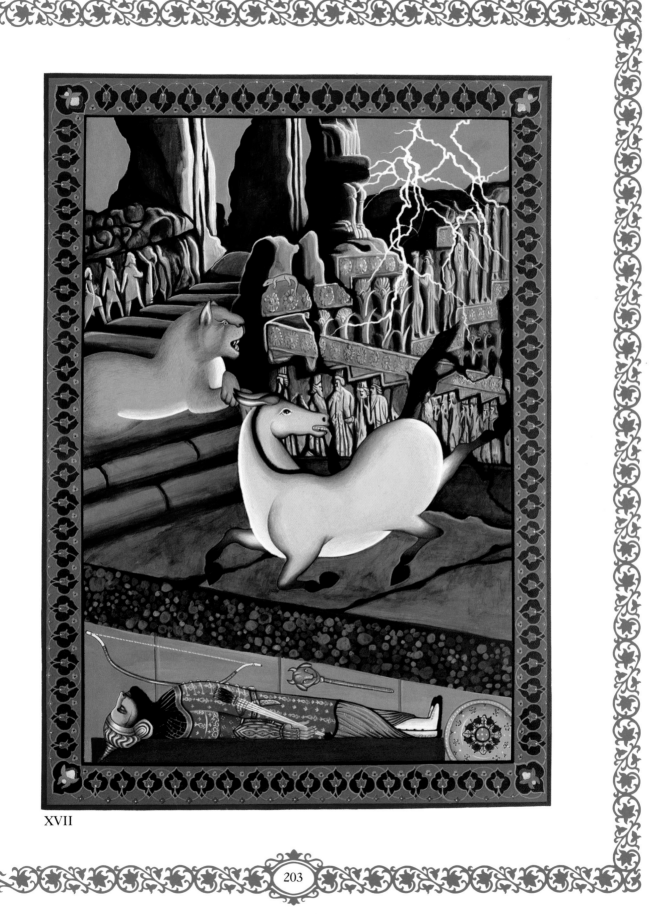

XVII

XX

XXI

Lo! some we loved, the loveliest and the best
That Time and Fate of all their Vintage prest,
 Have drunk their Cup a Round or two before,
And one by one crept silently to Rest.

XXII

And we, that now make merry in the Room
They left, and Summer dresses in new Bloom,
 Ourselves must we beneath the Couch of Earth
Descend, ourselves to make a Couch — for whom?

XXIII

Ah, make the most of what we yet may spend,
Before we too into the Dust descend;
 Dust into Dust, and under Dust, to lie,
Sans Wine, sans Song, sans Singer, and — sans End.

XXIV

Alike for those who for TO-DAY prepare,
And those that after a TO-MORROW stare,
 A Muezzin from the Tower of Darkness cries
"Fools! your Reward is neither Here nor There!"

XXV

Why, all the Saints and Sages who discuss'd
Of the Two Worlds so learnedly, are thrust
 Like foolish Prophets forth; their Words to Scorn
Are scatter'd, and their Mouths are stopt with Dust.

XXVI

Oh, come with old Khayyam, and leave the Wise
To talk; one thing is certain, that Life flies;
*   One thing is certain, and the Rest is Lies;*
The Flower that once has blown for ever dies.

XXVII

Myself when young did eagerly frequent
Doctor and Saint, and heard great Argument
*   About it and about: but evermore*
Came out by the same Door as in I went.

XXVIII

With them the Seed of Wisdom did I sow,
And with my own hand labour'd it to grow:
*   And this was all the Harvest that I reap'd —*
"I came like Water, and like Wind I go."

XXIX

Into the Universe, and why not knowing,
Nor whence, like Water willy-nilly flowing;
*   And out of it, as Wind along the Waste,*
I know not whither, willy-nilly blowing.

XXX

What, without asking, hither hurried whence?
And, without asking, whither hurried hence!
*   Another and another Cup to drown*
The Memory of this Impertinence!

XXVIII

XXXIII

XXXI

Up from Earth's Centre through the Seventh Gate
I rose, and on the Throne of Saturn sate,
    And many Knots unravel'd by the Road;
But not the Knot of Human Death and Fate.

XXXII

There was a Door to which I found no Key:
There was a Veil past which I could not see:
    Some little Talk awhile of ME and THEE
There seem'd — and then no more of THEE and ME.

XXXIII

Then to the rolling Heav'n itself I cried,
Asking, "What Lamp had Destiny to guide
    Her little Children stumbling in the Dark?"
And — "A blind Understanding!" Heav'n replied.

XXXIV

Then to this earthen Bowl did I adjourn
My Lip the secret Well of Life to learn:
    And Lip to Lip it murmur'd — "While you live
Drink! — for once dead you never shall return."

XXXV

I think the Vessel, that with fugitive
Articulation answer'd, once did live,
    And merry-make; and the cold Lip I kiss'd
How many Kisses might it take — and give!

XXXVI

For in the Market-place, one Dusk of Day,
I watch'd the Potter thumping his wet Clay:
    And with its all obliterated Tongue
It murmur'd — "Gently, Brother, gently, pray!"

XXXVII

Ah, fill the Cup: — what boots it to repeat
How Time is slipping underneath our Feet:
    Unborn TO-MORROW, and dead YESTERDAY
Why fret about them if TO-DAY be sweet!

XXXVIII

One Moment in Annihilation's Waste,
One Moment, of the Well of Life to taste —
    The Stars are setting and the Caravan
Starts for the Dawn of Nothing — Oh, make haste!

XXXIX

How long, how long, in Infinite Pursuit
Of This and That endeavour and dispute?
    Better be merry with the fruitful Grape
Than sadder after none, or bitter, Fruit.

XL

You know, my Friends, how long since in my House
For a new Marriage I did make Carouse:
    Divorced old barren Reason from my Bed,
And took the Daughter of the Vine to Spouse.

XLI

For "IS" and "IS-NOT" though with Rule and Line,
And, "UP-AND-DOWN" without, I could define,
    I yet in all I only cared to know,
Was never deep in anything but — Wine.

XLII

And lately, by the Tavern Door agape,
Came stealing through the Dusk an Angel Shape
    Bearing a Vessel on his Shoulder; and
He bid me taste of it; and 'twas — the Grape!

XLIII

The Grape that can with Logic absolute
The Two-and-Seventy jarring Sects confute:
    The subtle Alchemist that in a Trice
Life's leaden Metal into Gold transmute.

XLIV

The mighty Mahmud, the victorious Lord,
That all the misbelieving and black Horde
    Of Fears and Sorrows that infest the Soul
Scatters and slays with his enchanted Sword.

XLV

But leave the Wise to wrangle, and with me
The Quarrel of the Universe let be:
    And, in some corner of the Hubbub coucht,
Make Game of that which makes as much of Thee.

XLVI

For in and out, above, about, below,
'Tis nothing but a Magic Shadow-show
*   Play'd in a Box whose Candle is the Sun,*
Round which we Phantom Figures come and go.

XLVII

And if the Wine you drink, the Lip you press,
End in the Nothing all Things end in — Yes —
*   Then fancy while Thou art, Thou art but what*
Thou shalt be — Nothing — Thou shalt not be less.

XLVIII

While the Rose blows along the River Brink,
With old Khayyam the Ruby Vintage drink:
*   And when the Angel with his darker Draught*
Draws up to Thee — take that, and do not shrink.

XLIX

'Tis all a Chequer-board of Nights and Days
Where Destiny with Men for Pieces plays:
*   Hither and thither moves, and mates, and slays,*
And one by one back in the Closet lays.

L

The Ball no Question makes of Ayes and Noes,
But Right or Left as strikes the Player goes;
*   And He that toss'd Thee down into the Field,*
He knows about it all — HE knows — HE knows!

XLVIII

LI

The Moving Finger writes; and, having writ,
Moves on: nor all thy Piety nor Wit
    Shall lure it back to cancel half a Line,
Nor all thy Tears wash out a Word of it.

LII

And that inverted Bowl we call The Sky,
Whereunder crawling coop't we live and die,
    Lift not thy hands to It for help — for It
Rolls impotently on as Thou or I.

LIII

With Earth's first Clay They did the Last Man's knead,
And then of the Last Harvest sow'd the Seed:
    Yea, the first Morning of Creation wrote
What the Last Dawn of Reckoning shall read.

LIV

I tell Thee this — When, starting from the Goal,
Over the shoulders of the flaming Foal
    Of Heav'n and Parwin and Mushtara they flung,
In my predestined Plot of Dust and Soul.

LV

The Vine had struck a Fibre; which about
It clings my Being — let the Sufi flout;
    Of My Base Metal may be filed a Key,
That shall unlock the Door he howls without.

LVI

And this I know: whether the one True Light,
Kindle to Love, or Wrath consume me quite,
One glimpse of It within the Tavern caught
Better than in the Temple lost outright.

LVII

Oh, Thou, who didst with Pitfall and with Gin
Beset the Road I was to wander in,
Thou wilt not with Predestination round
Enmesh me, and impute my Fall to Sin?

LVIII

Oh, Thou, who Man of baser Earth didst make,
And who with Eden didst devise the Snake;
For all the Sin wherewith the Face of Man
Is blacken'd, Man's Forgiveness give — and take!

LIX

Listen again. One evening at the Close
Of Ramazan, ere the better Moon arose,
In that old Potter's Shop I stood alone
With the clay Population round in Rows.

LX

And, strange to tell, among the Earthen Lot
Some could articulate, while others not:
And suddenly one more impatient cried —
"Who is the Potter, pray, and who the Pot?"

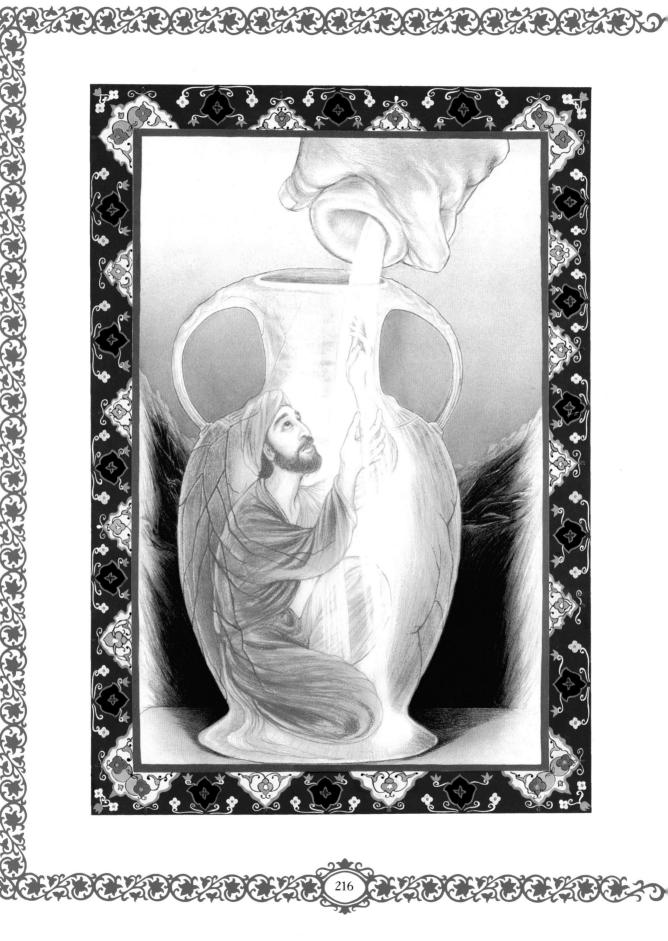

LXI

Then said another — "Surely not in vain
My Substance from the common Earth was ta'en,
    That He who subtly wrought me into Shape
Should stamp me back to common Earth again."

LXII

Another said — "Why, ne'er a peevish Boy,
Would break the Bowl from which he drank in Joy;
    Shall He that made the Vessel in pure Love
And Fancy, in an after Rage destroy!"

LXIII

None answer'd this; but after Silence spake
A Vessel of a more ungainly Make:
    "They sneer at me for leaning all awry;
What! did the Hand then of the Potter shake?"

LXIV

Said one — "Folks of a surly Tapster tell,
And daub his Visage with the Smoke of Hell;
    They talk of some strict Testing of us — Pish!
He's a Good Fellow, and 'twill all be well."

LXV

Then said another with a long-drawn Sigh,
"My Clay with long oblivion is gone dry:
    But, fill me with the old familiar Juice,
Methinks I might recover by-and-by!"

LXVI

So while the Vessels one by one were speaking,
One spied the little Crescent all were seeking:
    And then they jogg'd each other, "Brother, Brother!
Hark to the Porter's Shoulder-knot a-creaking!"

LXVII

Ah, with the Grape my fading Life provide,
And wash my Body whence the Life has died,
    And in a Windingsheet of Vine-leaf wrapt,
So bury me by some sweet Garden-side.

LXVIII

That ev'n my buried Ashes such a Snare
Of Perfume shall fling up into the Air,
    As not a True Believer passing by
But shall be overtaken unaware.

LXIX

Indeed, the Idols I have loved so long
Have done my Credit in Men's Eye much wrong:
    Have drown'd my Honour in a shallow Cup,
And sold my Reputation for a Song.

LXX

Indeed, indeed, Repentance oft before
I swore—but was I sober when I swore?
    And then and then came Spring, and Rose-in-hand
My thread-bare Penitence apieces tore.

LXXI

And much as Wine has play'd the Infidel,
And robb'd me of my Robe of Honour — well,
    I often wonder what the Vintners buy
One half so precious as the Goods they sell.

LXXII

Alas, that Spring should vanish with the Rose!
That Youth's sweet-scented Manuscript should close!
    The Nightingale that in the Branches sang,
Ah, whence, and whither flown again, who knows!

LXXIII

Ah, Love! could thou and I with Fate conspire
To grasp this sorry Scheme of Things entire,
    Would not we shatter it to bits — and then
Re-mould it nearer to the Heart's Desire!

LXXIV

Ah, Moon of my Delight, who know'st no wane,
The Moon of Heav'n is rising once again:
    How oft hereafter rising shall she look
Through this same Garden after me — in vain!

LXXV

And when Thyself with shining Foot shall pass
Among the Guests Star-scatter'd on the Grass,
    And in thy joyous Errand reach the Spot
Where I made one — turn down an empty Glass!

About the Author

"The ideal of love for God and service to humanity found full expression in the life of Paramahansa Yogananda.... Though the major part of his life was spent outside India, still he takes his place among our great saints. His work continues to grow and shine ever more brightly, drawing people everywhere on the path of the pilgrimage of the Spirit."

—from a tribute by the Government of India upon issuing a commemorative stamp in Paramahansa Yogananda's honor on the twenty-fifth anniversary of his passing

Paramahansa Yogananda was born Mukunda Lal Ghosh on January 5, 1893, in the north Indian city of Gorakhpur, at the foot of the Himalaya mountains. From his earliest years, it was clear that his life was marked for a divine destiny. According to those closest to him, even as a child the depth of his awareness and experience of the spiritual was far beyond the ordinary. In his youth he sought out many of India's sages and saints, hoping to find an illumined teacher to guide him in his spiritual quest.

It was in 1910, at the age of seventeen, that he met and became a disciple of the revered Swami Sri Yukteswar. In the hermitage of this great master of Yoga he spent the better part of the next ten years, receiving Sri Yukteswar's strict but loving spiritual discipline. After graduating from Calcutta University in 1915, he took formal vows as a monk of India's venerable monastic Swami Order, at which time he received the name Yogananda (signifying bliss, *ananda*, through divine union, *yoga*).

In 1917, Sri Yogananda began his life's work with the founding of a "how-to-live" school for boys, where modern educational methods were combined with yoga training and instruction in spiritual ideals. Three years later he was invited to serve as India's delegate to an International Congress of Religious Liberals convening in Boston. His address to the Congress, on "The Science of Religion," was enthusiastically received.

For the next several years, he lectured and taught on the East coast and in 1924 embarked on a cross-continental speaking tour. In Los Angeles, he began a two-month series of lectures and classes in January of 1925. As elsewhere, his talks were greeted with interest and acclaim. The *Los Angeles Times* reported: "The Philharmonic Auditorium presents the extraordinary spectacle of thousands...being turned away an hour before the advertised opening of a lecture with the 3000-seat hall filled to its utmost capacity."

Later that year, Sri Yogananda established in Los Angeles an international headquarters of Self-Realization Fellowship, the society he had founded in 1920 to disseminate his teachings on the ancient science and philosophy of Yoga and its time-honored methods of meditation.* Over the next decade, he traveled extensively, speaking in major cities throughout the country. Among those who became his stu-

---

* The specific path of meditation and God-communion taught by Paramahansa Yogananda is known as *Kriya Yoga*, a sacred spiritual science originating millenniums ago in India. Sri Yogananda's *Autobiography of a Yogi* provides a general introduction to the philosopy and methods of *Kriya Yoga;* detailed instruction in the techniques is made available to qualified students of his *Self-Realization Fellowship Lessons.*

dents were many prominent figures in science, business, and the arts, including horticulturist Luther Burbank; Metropolitan Opera soprano Amelita Galli-Curci; Margaret Wilson, daughter of President Woodrow Wilson; poet Edwin Markham; and symphony conductor Leopold Stokowski.

After an eighteen-month tour of Europe and India in 1935–36, he began to withdraw somewhat from his nationwide public lecturing so as to devote himself to building an enduring foundation for his worldwide work and to the writings that would carry his message to future generations. His life story, *Autobiography of a Yogi,* was published in 1946. In continuous publication ever since, it has been translated into many languages and has gained renown as a modern spiritual classic.

Today, the spiritual and humanitarian work begun by Paramahansa Yogananda is being carried on under the direction of Sri Daya Mata, one of his earliest and closest disciples and president of Self-Realization Fellowship/Yogoda Satsanga Society of India since 1955.* In addition to publishing Paramahansa Yogananda's lectures, writings, and informal talks—including a comprehensive series of *Self-Realization Fellowship Lessons* for home study—the society guides Self-Realization members in their practice of Sri Yogananda's teachings; oversees its temples, retreats, and meditation centers around the world, as well as the monastic communities of the Self-Realization Order; and coordinates the Worldwide Prayer Circle, which serves as an instrument to help bring healing to those in physical, mental, or spiritual need and greater harmony among the nations.

Since his passing in 1952, Paramahansa Yogananda has come to be recognized as one of the truly great spiritual figures of the twentieth century. Through his universal teachings and exemplary life, he has helped people of all races, cultures, and creeds to realize and express more fully in their own lives the beauty and nobility of the human spirit. In a tribute of appreciation, author and educator Dr. Wendell Thomas wrote: "I came to [Paramahansa] Yogananda many years ago, not as a seeker or devotee, but as a writer with a sympathetic yet analytic and critical approach. Happily, I found in Yoganandaji a rare combination. While steadfast in the ancient principles of his profound faith, he had the gift of generous adaptability....With his quick wit and great spirit he was well fitted to promote reconciliation and truth among the religious seekers of the world. He brought peace and joy to multitudes."

---

* In India Paramahansa Yogananda's work is known as Yogoda Satsanga Society.

PARAMAHANSA YOGANANDA:
A YOGI IN LIFE AND DEATH

Paramahansa Yogananda entered *mahasamadhi* (a yogi's final conscious exit from the body) in Los Angeles, California, on March 7, 1952, after concluding his speech at a banquet held in honor of H.E. Binay R. Sen, Ambassador of India.

The great world teacher demonstrated the value of yoga (scientific techniques for God-realization) not only in life but in death. Weeks after his departure his unchanged face shone with the divine luster of incorruptibility.

Mr. Harry T. Rowe, Los Angeles Mortuary Director, Forest Lawn Memorial-Park (in which the body of the great master is temporarily placed), sent Self-Realization Fellowship a notarized letter from which the following extracts are taken:

"The absence of any visual signs of decay in the dead body of Paramahansa Yogananda offers the most extraordinary case in our experience....No physical disintegration was visible in his body even twenty days after death....No indication of mold was visible on his skin, and no visible desiccation (drying up) took place in the bodily tissues. This state of perfect preservation of a body is, so far as we know from mortuary annals, an unparalleled one....At the time of receiving Yogananda's body, the Mortuary personnel expected to observe, through the glass lid of the casket, the usual progressive signs of bodily decay. Our astonishment increased as day followed day without bringing any visible change in the body under observation. Yogananda's body was apparently in a phenomenal state of immutability....

"No odor of decay emanated from his body at any time....The physical appearance of Yogananda on March 27th, just before the bronze cover of the casket was put into position, was the same as it had been on March 7th. He looked on March 27th as fresh and as unravaged by decay as he had looked on the night of his death. On March 27th there was no reason to say that his body had suffered any visible physical disintegration at all. For these reasons we state again that the case of Paramahansa Yogananda is unique in our experience."

AIMS AND IDEALS
of
Self-Realization Fellowship

As set forth by Paramahansa Yogananda, Founder

Sri Daya Mata, President

To disseminate among the nations a knowledge of definite scientific techniques for attaining direct personal experience of God.

To teach that the purpose of life is the evolution, through self-effort, of man's limited mortal consciousness into God Consciousness; and to this end to establish Self-Realization Fellowship temples for God-communion throughout the world, and to encourage the establishment of individual temples of God in the homes and in the hearts of men.

To reveal the complete harmony and basic oneness of original Christianity as taught by Jesus Christ and original Yoga as taught by Bhagavan Krishna; and to show that these principles of truth are the common scientific foundation of all true religions.

To point out the one divine highway to which all paths of true religious beliefs eventually lead: the highway of daily, scientific, devotional meditation on God.

To liberate man from his threefold suffering: physical disease, mental inharmonies, and spiritual ignorance.

To encourage "plain living and high thinking"; and to spread a spirit of brotherhood among all peoples by teaching the eternal basis of their unity: kinship with God.

To demonstrate the superiority of mind over body, of soul over mind.

To overcome evil by good, sorrow by joy, cruelty by kindness, ignorance by wisdom.

To unite science and religion through realization of the unity of their underlying principles.

To advocate cultural and spiritual understanding between East and West, and the exchange of their finest distinctive features.

To serve mankind as one's larger Self.

Other Books by
PARAMAHANSA YOGANANDA

Available at bookstores or directly from the publisher:

Self-Realization Fellowship • 3880 San Rafael Avenue
Los Angeles, California 90065

Autobiography of a Yogi
Man's Eternal Quest
The Divine Romance
Where There Is Light: *Insight and Inspiration*
for Meeting Life's Challenges
The Science of Religion
Whispers from Eternity
Songs of the Soul
Sayings of Paramahansa Yogananda
Scientific Healing Affirmations
How You Can Talk With God
Metaphysical Meditations
The Law of Success
Cosmic Chants

Audio recordings of informal talks by Paramahansa Yogananda

Beholding the One in All
Awake in the Cosmic Dream
The Great Light of God

Other books from the same publisher:

The Holy Science *by Swami Sri Yukteswar*
"Only Love" *by Sri Daya Mata*
Finding the Joy Within You: Personal Counsel for God-Centered Living
by Sri Daya Mata
God Alone: The Life and Letters of a Saint *by Sri Gyanamata*
"Mejda": The Family and the Early Life of Paramahansa Yogananda
by Sananda Lal Ghosh

Please request current catalog of books
and audio/video recordings before ordering.

Free Introductory Booklet: *Undreamed-of Possibilities*

The scientific techniques of meditation referred to in *Wine of the Mystic*, including *Kriya Yoga*, are taught in the *Self-Realization Fellowship Lessons*. For further information please write for the free introductory booklet *Undreamed-of Possibilities*.